# SEVEN STATES OF CONSCIOUSNESS

(Photo © Fred den Ouden, Amsterdam)

MAHARISHI MAHESH YOGI

# SEVEN STATES OF CONSCIOUSNESS:

*A vision of possibilities
suggested by the teaching of
Maharishi Mahesh Yogi*

by

ANTHONY CAMPBELL

LONDON
VICTOR GOLLANCZ LTD
1974

© Anthony Campbell 1973

ISBN 0 575 01659 0

First published June 1973

Second impression October 1973
Third impression May 1974

Printed in Great Britain
by Ebenezer Baylis and Son Limited
The Trinity Press, Worcester, and London

*To Pari*
*who always knew there must be a way*

# Acknowledgements

I wish to thank the following people for kindly allowing me to quote from material in which they hold the copyright.

*The Nature of Life*, by C. H. Waddington, George Allen & Unwin Ltd.; *Hindu and Muslim Mysticism*, by R. C. Zaehner, Athlone Press, University of London, publishing on behalf of the School of Oriental & African Studies; *Ecstasy: A Study of Some Secular and Religious Experiences*, by Marghanita Laski, Barrie & Jenkins Ltd.; *Sudden Religious Conversions in Temporal Lobe Epilepsy*, by Kenneth Dewhurst and A. W. Beard, the Editor of *The British Journal of Psychiatry* and Dr K. Dewhurst; *Mind and Matter* and *What is Life?*, by Erwin Schrödinger; *Man On His Nature*, by Sir Charles Sherrington, Cambridge University Press; *Mysticism Sacred and Profane*, by R. C. Zaehner, by permission of the Clarendon Press, © 1957 Oxford University Press; *Migraine*, by Oliver W. Sacks, extracts reprinted by permission of Faber & Faber Ltd.; *Mysticism and Philosophy*, by W. T. Stace, extracts reprinted by permission of Macmillan, London and Basingstoke; *Mysticism*, by Evelyn Underhill, Methuen & Co. Ltd.; *Diseases of the Nervous System*, by Lord Brain, *The Tibetan Book of the Great Liberation*, edited by W. Y. Evans-Wents, Oxford University Press; Quotations from the Upanishads are from *The Upanishads*, trans. Juan Mascaró, copyright © Juan Mascaró, 1965, reprinted by permission of Penguin Books Ltd.; *Psychological Commentary on the Tibetan Book of the Great Liberation*, by C. G. Jung (reprinted in *The Collected Works of C. G. Jung*, vol. 11, *Psychology and Religion: West and East*), *Religion, Philosophy, and Psychical Research*, by C. D. Broad, Routledge & Kegan Paul Ltd.; *The Neurophysiological Aspects of Hallucinations and Illusory Experience*, by W. Grey Walter, the Editor of the *Journal* and *Proceedings* of the Society for Psychical Research; *The Spiritual Letters of Dom John Chapman*, edited by Dom Roger Hudleston, Sheed & Ward Ltd.; *Brain and Conscious Experience*, edited by J. C. Eccles, Springer-Verlag, New York, 1966; *Altered States of Consciousness*, edited by Charles T. Tart, John Wiley & Sons Inc.

The quotations on pp. 140–1 and 142–3 from 'The Creativeness of Life' by E. W. Sinnott first appeared in *Creativity and its Cultivation* ed. H. H. Anderson, Harper, 1959. Quotations on pp. 124–7 and 144–5 from the work of Walter N. Pahnke and William A. Richards first appeared in *The Journal of Religion and Health*, vol. 5, 1966, pp. 175–208, published by the Academy of Religion and Mental Health, 16E. 34th St, New York 10016.

## Contents

# Introduction

In 1967 I began the practice of transcendental meditation, and in this book I have tried to set down some of the insights which resulted. I must emphasize at the outset that the book is frankly personal; I have not primarily intended to write an exposition of the philosophy underlying the meditation, for the very good reason that this has already been done by Maharishi himself; and for anyone else to think of adding to what he has written would be ludicrous. My aim has rather been to show how the practice of the meditation itself, and study of the ideas underlying it, have shed light on a number of problems which had long perplexed me. My hope is that what I have written may be of interest to other people who have been thinking on similar lines to myself.

I cannot emphasize too strongly that the way in which I have chosen to approach my subject is simply one of an almost infinite number of ways that might be used. Maharishi himself has from time to time presented his ideas from different angles; in the last couple of years, for example, he has given more weight to the notion of creativity and has been speaking in terms of the 'Science of Creative Intelligence'; this has allowed him to develop a non-religious terminology in which to set out his philosophy. Since, however, one of my principal aims in this book has been to explore in the light of his teaching the common ground that appears to me to exist between science and religion, I have drawn mainly upon his earlier published writings (*The Science of Being and Art of Living* and the *Commentary on the Bhagavad Gita*) and have adopted the terminology which he uses there.

Whatever course one chooses, language is bound to remain a problem since there is no neutral vocabulary to name religious concepts. Even 'meditation' itself is a case in point; Maharishi has often said that, had he known the disrepute into which the word had fallen in the West, he would have called his technique by another name. So perhaps it would be best to start by trying to define transcendental meditation.

A brief and reasonably comprehensive description would be: a simple natural technique for the progressive refinement of the nervous system through the regular alternation of deep rest and activity. Notice what it is *not*: it is not a religion, a philosophy, or a way of life—though it has relevance to all of these.

Historically, the meditation has been made available in our time by Maharishi Mahesh Yogi, who in turn attributes his inspiration to his own master. For Maharishi was the closest disciple of a renowned Indian teacher, Swami Brahmananda Sarasvati (1869–1953). For most of his life Swami Brahmananda was a strict recluse, but for the last thirteen years or so he was prevailed upon to become Shankaracharya of Jyotir Math, in the Himalayas. (Jyotir Math is one of four monasteries, or seats of learning, founded by the original Shankaracharya, who is believed by most modern scholars to have lived about A.D. 800.) After his master's death Maharishi remained for two years in solitude and then began to teach. He inaugurated the Spiritual Regeneration Movement on a world-wide basis on 31st December 1957, and since then it has spread so rapidly that today many thousands of people are practising transcendental meditation and few countries lack at least one centre for instruction in the technique. (See the Postscript for further details.)

Transcendental meditation is thus simultaneously new and old. So far as I am aware, it is unlike any other method of 'meditation' being taught today; yet Maharishi comes from a very ancient tradition. Maharishi himself insists that a similar technique, founded on the same essential insight, must have been at the basis of all the great religions of the past. That this is true of Buddhism seems to me very likely; whether it is so true of Christianity I do not know. Certainly the existence of a powerful spiritual technique among the early Christians would go far to explain the remarkable success of their religion, and it is also true that one can find evidence in the New Testament which seems to support a view of this kind; but whether an adequate case for this hypothesis can really be made out is a question I must leave to Biblical scholars.

However this may be, when one turns to the later development of Christianity one undoubtedly does find in the monastic tradition a wealth of fascinating practices which have affinities with transcendental meditation. I shall have more to say about this later.

Maharishi's view (which is in line with that of the Bhagavad Gita) is that the knowledge of how to contact one's inner depths has existed from time to time in the past, but has inevitably become obscured with the passage of time. His message is therefore one of 'revival'. Certainly, when one practises transcendental meditation it becomes easy to understand how the secret could become lost; for the meditation is so delicate (even though 'natural') that the slightest deviation upsets it completely. Subtract or add anything, and nothing happens at all. And once the correct practice is lost, people try, vainly, to produce by conscious effort what formerly occurred spontaneously.

Transcendental meditation is complete in itself. Being entirely practical, it does not depend upon belief or acceptance of theories; all that is needed for successful practice is a simple willingness to experiment. Indeed, a certain degree of scepticism is quite a valuable asset at the outset, for it prevents one from looking too eagerly for results and so spoiling the naturalness of the process.

However, I have already referred to the philosophy underlying transcendental meditation. Where does this come from, and on what is it based?

In one sense it is true to say that these ideas are Indian. Maharishi, after all, has an Indian background and the meditation itself comes from that source. In another sense, however, this may be misleading; for the ideas, as I hope to show, are not merely Indian but are universal; that is, they stem from a direct insight into the nature of man and his relation to the universe that arises as a result of reaching a clearer state of awareness.

It is vital to understand that these ideas cannot be fully grasped except by someone whose psycho-physical organism has been suitably prepared for them. A merely intellectual assent to propositions is by no means enough. (Plato, it seems, envisaged a physical as well as a mental preparation for the study of philosophy.) These considerations are important if one wishes to import Indian teachings to the West—a currently fashionable pre-occupation. For, as I have said, the knowledge of transcendental meditation has apparently long been missing from India, and hence although the ancient Indian writings such as the Upanishads do give profoundly moving accounts of the nature of reality that have influenced a number of important Western thinkers, their real significance is not appreciated today either in the West or in the East. They are like inscriptions in some ancient tongue of which only a little is known.

The Westerner, therefore, should not feel that he is being asked to swallow a lot of 'Indian' notions—which, moreover, a contemplation of the defects of modern Indian society might make him the more inclined to reject. Maharishi may indeed, as he claims, have revived truth rather than discovered it; but the erosion of time has been so complete that his teachings today are scarcely less of a novelty to Indians than they are to the West.

However, this argument may not suffice for everyone. If I am not mistaken, a number of readers will take up this book with a fair amount of suspicion. 'Here', they will say to themselves, 'is another foolish Westerner who has been taken in by a specious Eastern guru.'

The suspicion is understandable. Our age has seen many false prophets deified by their foolish worshippers. Surely a rational man will find all such 'enthusiasms' abhorrent, and, even if by mischance he finds himself attracted to one of these figures, prevent himself from being swept away by throwing out the sheet anchors of intellectual scepticism and historical awareness?

Such criticism is, I believe, due to a double misunderstanding. Part of the confusion arises because of differences between the Eastern and Western concepts of the philosopher. For us in the West a philosopher is not necessarily a wise man; he is a professional thinker, which is not quite the same thing. In traditional Indian thought, on the other hand, the philosopher is the knower of reality. The distinction goes back at least as far as Descartes, with his principle of systematic doubt. Maharishi has summed up the difference neatly by saying that in the West the philosopher thinks of himself as an ignorant man who tries to reach the truth by the exercise of his reason, while in India the philosopher is an enlightened man who brings truth to the ignorant. Plainly there are here two irreconcilable approaches, and to use the word 'philosophy' for both is misleading. For us, of course, the very idea of a man handing down truth as it were from above is repellent; it smacks of a religious authoritarianism we have decisively rejected. (Maharishi, however, rejects it just as firmly.) Many have even abandoned the idea of truth itself; Pontius Pilate has had many followers.

Now, I have to admit that my experience of meditation has led me to believe that the state of enlightenment does exist, and if this is so it must afford a standpoint from which ultimate truth can be discerned. Maharishi, then, is a man who has a true vision of reality, and he describes this in language that he hopes will make sense to the rest of us who lack this vision. The enlightened man is the prisoner who has escaped from Plato's cave and returned with news of the outside world. I do not mean to say that Maharishi is the only such returned prisoner; no doubt there have been, and still are, others in both East and West; but Maharishi is unique in that he can not only tell travellers' tales to the half-incredulous prisoners still chained within, but he has the key to unlock their chains. More than that, he knows that the prisoners are stiff from long sitting, and that the light outside will dazzle them at first. And therefore he has worked out a scheme for gradually exercising their newly unfettered limbs and for allowing their weak eyes to become progressively better adapted to the light of the sun. It is in his understanding of the problems that confront the 'ignorant' that his great originality as a teacher lies.

The other cause of misunderstanding also has its origin in the difference between Eastern and the Western traditions. For Indians, 'enlightenment' occurs as the result of personal devotion to the master. The disciple is expected to serve the master by day and night, learning to anticipate his every wish, his likes and dislikes. In this way enlightenment grows in the disciple by a sort of spiritual osmosis.

Now, this tradition clearly cannot be the basis of a world-wide movement at the present day. For one thing, it is unsuited to the instruction of large numbers of people; genuine masters are few at the best of times, and the number of disciples who can serve any one master is obviously limited. But in any case the Western character is unsuited to the master-disciple relationship; we find it, as a rule, incompatible with our tradition of personal independence. It is, I think, a measure of Maharishi's originality and grasp of essentials that he has seen this and adapted his approach accordingly. Transcendental meditation, though taught individually, does not depend on devotion to a master, any more than on assent to dogma. Thus there is nothing in the practice of this meditation to offend the susceptibilities of even the most morbidly independent Westerner. And for me at least this freedom and lack of 'commitment' were quite essential inducements when I first started to meditate.

Which brings me to the question, how I began to practise transcendental meditation. This is something I am often asked, and I feel that in a book of this kind an answer to the question is necessary; it will help the reader to have as clear an idea as may be of my general frame of reference, so that he may know what kind of animal he is dealing with. There are few experiences more frustrating than reading something which interests one on a topic like this without knowing anything definite about the author's general background and assumptions. True, one can glean a good deal by reading between the lines, but it creates a feeling of uncertainty, like having to read a map without knowing the scale.

At the time I first heard of transcendental meditation I was in a state of agnosticism which it had cost me a fair amount of effort to achieve. I was brought up as a Roman Catholic, and went to Downside, where the atmosphere, though profoundly religious, was liberal and intellectual. Emphasis was laid on intelligent understanding of the faith, and by the time I left school I was a convinced, indeed an enthusiastic, Catholic.

Unlike some adolescents, I underwent no specifically religious awakening. My attitude to religion was, I think, that of most of my school contemporaries: a sort of complacent security that we were right. We *knew*, and the rest of the world did not. At Easter each year a retreat was held, and was usually conducted by some invited speaker from outside the community. In my last year this office was filled by a Jesuit, who spoke to us senior boys about the glory and excitement of going out into the world to bring it back to the faith. This idea thoroughly took hold of me, and I began to long for the time, soon to come, when I should be able to start convincing the unregenerate masses of the truth of Catholicism. Indeed, the question that puzzled me was why, the truth being so self-evident, everyone had not become Catholic long ago. We were so obviously right!

Since then, I suppose, the wheel has all but come full circle. As J. M. Cohen has pointed out, we tread a spiral path.

Yet even while I was still at school there were doubts—or difficulties, as the headmaster insisted on calling them. For one thing, the idea that all religions were different paths to, or versions of, a single truth was one that held a deep attraction for me, even though it was of course frequently anathematized in classes of religious instruction. I never voiced it to anyone, even my closest friends, but its inherent reasonableness never failed to strike me.

Another difficulty arose when the headmaster said, with a burst of hearty laughter: 'People talk of the mystery of the meaning of life. For you, of course, there is no mystery; the meaning of life is plain.' But I had a Romantic longing for mystery. The infinite vastness of space, the '*silence de ces espaces eternels*', sometimes frightened me, as it had Pascal, and the catechismal question and answer routine ('Who made me?' 'God made me.' 'Why did God make me?' 'God made me to know him, love him, and serve him in this world, and to be happy with him for ever in the next') while it satisfied me intellectually, left me cold emotionally.

This was not a new development for me. When I was quite a small child, I used to lie awake at night and wonder why God had made anything at all. The mere fact that something existed rather than nothing seemed an inexpressibly great mystery, and one that could not be conjured away by a formula. Instinctively I felt that it was something I should have to come to terms with sooner or later.

I remained a convinced Catholic—at least on the conscious level—for some three years after leaving school, even though during this time I was undergoing a period of unusually intense and prolonged adolescent turmoil. Not until I was living in Madrid, after completing my National Service, did I find that I no longer was a Catholic or even a Christian. The eventual discovery was quite sudden. It happened that among the small foreign community in Madrid at the time (this was 1955) was

Chris, a Downside contemporary of mine. At school we had hardly known each other, for we were in different houses and moreover Chris was a year older than me, but now we found we had much in common. Chris at this time was undergoing acute doubts about religion, and we used to have long arguments, I taking the part of the superior and slightly cocksure defender of the faith. But suddenly I found that not only was I failing to convince Chris; I was not even convincing myself.

It is difficult to describe what happened in a logical, step-by-step fashion, because it was not like that. I did not start by having specific doubts which gradually grew; rather, my religious opinions underwent a sudden reversal at all points simultaneously. I suppose that over the preceding years my belief in Christianity had been fading away at an unconscious level, like a building attacked by termites; outwardly all seemed well, but inwardly the destruction was proceeding apace, until eventually a mere shell was left that crumbled at a touch. Once started, the collapse did not stop until everything was lost; the whole process did not take more than a few days. Papal infallibility was first to go, I think; it was followed in rapid sequence by the Apostolic succession, the Virgin Birth, the resurrection, and the divinity of Christ. The existence of God Himself may have endured a day or two longer, but soon that too followed the rest.

Within a few days I had gone much further than Chris himself. Curiously, my first sensations were of great relief and freedom. The mystery of life was now indeed fully open to me to explore. I could start at the beginning.

But a Catholic upbringing is not so easily shaken off; and about a year later, when I was married and a medical student in Dublin, I began to be haunted by the fear that I had made a mistake in rejecting Catholicism, in which case, presumably, I should go to hell. I suffered from nightmares, and became afraid of death. Pari, my Persian wife, had to put up with long theological discussions of problems which she, as an agnostic ex-Moslem, naturally found difficult to resolve.

Such a state of mind will probably seem incomprehensible or pathological to many people. Religion is increasingly a this-wordly affair nowadays, and it may appear incredible that a reasonably intelligent and educated medical student in the middle of the twentieth century should be deeply affected by such irrational fears. After all, my religious upbringing had, as I have said, been relatively liberal; I do not think I had to listen to a single hell-fire sermon, and many of the monks who taught me had been intellectually highly sophisticated. Yet it was the very reasonableness of Catholicism as I knew it that made its rejection so painful. If it had been taught to me by unimaginative bigots I should have found no difficulty in dropping it, but as it was I was forced to controvert and discount the conclusions of some subtle and original minds, many of whose attitudes and presuppositions on other subjects I still shared. Catholicism was for me much more than a relic of childhood superstitition; it was a whole climate of thought, a way of looking at the world. It was easy to say that the Downside monks, though highly intelligent and cultured men, were blinded by their preconceptions. This was doubtless true; but that argument cut both ways. What guarantee had I that my own thinking was any more free from sources of error of which I was quite unaware?

I do not think I ever became a full-blooded atheist. At times I came near to believing that the world was an accident, yet always I was stopped by the sheer improbability of the idea. My position thus remained a vague deism; I *sensed*, rather than believed, that, as Victoria Sackville-West has put it, 'there is only one comprehensive, stupendous unity of which we apprehend but the smallest fragment' (*Saint Joan of Arc*, Penguin, p. 382). Certainly I did not think of this unity as in any way personal. It was not something to pray to, or to take refuge in in time of trouble; it was simply there.

Of course, my worries about religion did not always remain at the same pitch of intensity. Gradually they died away, and by the time I qualified they had ceased to trouble me almost completely. Yet though religion itself was fading away throughout the time I was a medical student, the questions which it was supposed to answer remained as real to me as ever. Indeed, they became more real. This, I am sure, was an individual peculiarity. Many people more sensitive and intelligent than myself would have been perfectly content to remain as vague agnostics. I could not do this. The ultimate questions might be unanswerable, but I could not stop asking them on that score. I therefore started to look for an answer in the only place I knew: books.

I suppose it was natural that in this frame of mind I should have been attracted by Buddhism. I had already become interested in it as a result of reading Aldous Huxley (this was before Zen and psychedelic drugs became fashionable) and now I went into the subject in more detail with the help of Christmas Humphreys. If I had been living in London I should almost certainly have practised Buddhist meditation, but (fortunately, as I now see) there was no Buddhist centre in Dublin. However, I thought of myself as more or less a Buddhist for several years. What I liked about Buddhism, at least as refracted through Christmas Humphreys, was its insistence on thinking for oneself and on the importance of direct experience.

Nevertheless I was not entirely convinced. The essence of Buddhism, evidently, regardless of sect or school, was Nirvana. To reach Nirvana, to attain Buddhahood, was obviously wonderful beyond words—if it was possible. But here I ran up against the same problem I had encountered with Christianity. There is room for infinite argument about the character and actions, and even the existence, of Jesus. This is even more true of the Buddha, for the Pali Canon, on which our knowledge of the historical Gautama rests, was not written down until some six hundred years after the time to which it refers. It was easy to believe that there had lived a great religious teacher in India in the sixth century BC who was held by his followers to be 'enlightened', but that scarcely guaranteed the reality of enlightenment as a goal any more than the Apostles' Creed guaranteed the divinity of Christ. A more practical question was whether anyone was enlightened now. Clearly it was impossible to know, but I had a strong suspicion—based on no very good evidence, to be sure—that so-called enlightenment was a subjective state resulting from some form of self-hypnosis. I am aware that all these arguments were fairly naive, but at the time I was unable to go any further.

Pari, however, was wiser than I. She had a conviction that the Buddha's enlightenment was real, and that since he had found a path, a path must exist. Oddly enough, as a small girl she had the ambition to become a yogi, whom she pictured as a half-naked figure with birds nesting in his beard and plants growing in his upheld hand!

But there was another difficulty about Buddhism. Its most basic assumption seemed to be that existence was an evil. Even the pleasures of life were to be despised because they were fleeting and enmeshed one ever deeper in the world. The only hope lay in renunciation.

In this, of course, the Buddhists were at one with almost all the religious teachers of the West as well as the East. Certainly it seemed logical to hold that to attain the supreme goal of Nirvana one must accept the ideal of complete renunciation. Yet the middle-of-the-road Benedictines had brought me up to believe that the legitimate pleasures of life could and should be enjoyed as gifts of God. And the beauty of the world was so great. . . .

Having reached more or less a dead end with Buddhism, I tried other directions. Strangely enough, I knew almost nothing at this time about Hinduism; I had not even read the Upanishads or Bhagavad Gita. I think this was because I felt unable to cope mentally with the luxuriant confusion of Hinduism. Buddhism seemed an altogether more manageable affair.

I had never been greatly interested in psychoanalysis (an admission which will doubtless bring a knowing smile to the lips of any analyst who chances to read this) but now I read Jung's books in some depth. I found them difficult and often baffling, intensely fascinating, and ultimately frustrating. That Jung had immense wisdom was obvious; he was a visionary, whose theories gave me, I felt, a great deal of insight into myself. Yet he had an irritating streak of caution that time and again stopped him just when I was expecting some final over-whelming revelation about the nature of the soul, life after death, or the existence of God. Quite recently, when I read his introduction to the *Tibetan Book of the Great Liberation*, I understood rather better why this was. Jung had, I think, divined part of the truth—hence the fascination he often exerts on writers and artists generally—but, not surprisingly, he had not gone all the way, and as a result his thought lacked a foundation. (See pp. 62–63.)

While in Dublin I read J. B. Rhine's *Reach of the Mind*, and thus was led to take a lasting interest in psychical research. In Dublin few books on this were available, but when I came to London on my return from Persia I became a member of the Society for Psychical Research and embarked on a course of fairly intensive reading. I found this a liberating experience. There is room for endless dispute about the significance of the facts that have been revealed by psychical research in the nearly eighty years that have elapsed since the foundation of the Society, but I do not believe that anyone who takes the trouble to read even a small part of the accumulated evidence can avoid reaching the conclusion that the view of the world held by almost everyone who has been brought up within, or under the influence of, Western industrial society is gravely defective. (This, I suppose, is why so few people do look at the evidence.) The conviction that this was so caused me both exhilaration and alarm—alarm because I felt myself being driven into an intellectual quagmire. If the prevalent scientific world-view was wrong, what should I put in its place? Theosophy or anthroposophy perhaps? I found all such esoteric systems grotesque and repellent, though this was doubtless in part a reflection of my own intellectual priggishness, for I knew little about them; and had I been aware that anthroposophy had satisfied so subtle a thinker as Owen Barfield, I might well have given it serious consideration.

In this frame of mind I was heartened by reading C. D. Broad's magnificent *Lectures on Psychical Research*. This masterly survey by one of the most eminent of contemporary British philosophers not only reviews some of the most important material but attempts to fit it into some sort of coherent conceptual framework (though in the nature of the case this attempt can only be tentative). It is an extraordinary reflection of our inability to tolerate new ideas that this book is not better known, and I can only advise anyone who has not read it to do so.

Broad does not confine himself to the relatively well-established phenomena of telepathy, clairvoyance, and pre-cognition. He is bold enough to tackle head-on the least soluble of all the problems raised by psychical research: do we in any sense survive bodily death, and if so, what form might that survival conceivably take?

The available evidence seems to point inescapably to one of two conclusions: either survival is a reality, or else telepathy and clairvoyance can occur on a far more extensive scale than there is any warrant for from laboratory work. Before reading Broad I had preferred the second hypothesis, for the physiological evidence that our minds depend wholly on the existence of our brains seems quite overwhelming. Yet, as Broad (and others) have made clear, there is also quite strong evidence that survival does occur. Broad himself dislikes the idea of personal survival, but his final assessment of the position leads him to say: 'I should be slightly more annoyed than surprised if I should find myself in some sense persisting immediately after the death of my physical body. One can only wait and see, or alternatively (which is no less likely) wait and not see.' (*Lectures on Psychical Research*, p. 430.)[1]

I found the survival question absorbing. It seemed to me by far the most important problem facing psychical research. This was also the view of the founders of the Society for Psychical Research, but in recent years it appears to have attracted much less attention, perhaps in part because less evidence has been coming in. I think my Catholic upbringing played a part in making me feel as I did about survival, for Catholicism, unlike some other branches of Christianity, has remained largely other-worldly. To believe that this life is not all there is gives

---

[1] The form that survival might take was another matter. Prompted by Jung's interest, I read the *Tibetan Book of the Dead*, and found it uncomfortably convincing. It has clearly influenced H. H. Price's speculations on survival. As Broad points out, there is no guarantee that survival, if it occurs, is necessarily a pleasant affair. The Tibetans, of course, assume the reality of reincarnation, which has had a surprisingly good press among Western philosophers from Plato onwards and has recently received remarkable evidential support in Ian Stevenson's scholarly classic, *Twenty Cases Suggestive of Reincarnation*—another of those books whose implications are so far-reaching and revolutionary that they remain almost unknown.

one a feeling of security and hope that is perhaps fully appreciated only when it is lost.

It is easy to say that the longing for survival is merely selfish, and that the belief in a life after death reflects an inability to face reality. We, in our scientific age, know better than to dream such foolish dreams, the argument runs; the only immortality we can reasonably ask for is to live for a little while in the memories of our friends and to leave the world an iota better than when we came into it.

Perhaps so. But, realistically or not, I found myself as time went on increasingly in a frame of mind which has been most beautifully expressed by Freya Stark: 'So far as my personal object in life goes, I should wish to attain two things: First, the confidence of more time, not to be confined within the narrow limits of one life; secondly, the sense of death as a new and wonderful adventure. If these two can attain to a real sense of certainty, my own inner life will have succeeded—and I hope to succeed. It will mean the absolute liberation from fear, which is a form of slavery.' (*Beyond Euphrates*, p. 40.)

The seeking for a way to this liberation from fear became my guiding principle. Yet I had no idea how to attain it. The liberation I sought must, to be worth anything, be proof against not only death but also physical pain. For to reconcile oneself to the fact of pain seems to me probably the most difficult task of all. A convinced atheist can die with dignity, like Hume; extinction can certainly be faced. But in this age which has seen deliberate, and almost completely successful, attempts to create literal hell on earth, no one can be safe within the armour of his own integrity who has not established himself on some reality which is not accessible to the torturers. And, given the apparently one-sided dependence of the mind on the body, what could that reality be? Something analogous to the soul seemed to me the only possibility.

It is easy to say that to seek such a reality warps one's judgement, and that one finds what one looks for. But it seems to me that the wilful refusal even to consider the possibility of survival—a much commoner attitude today—is equally warping. What is needed is scepticism, in the correct sense of the word. At all events, the conclusion which I reached at this time was that, although the philosophical arguments for survival were worthless (Broad has called them 'philosophical fluff'), the possibility of some form of survival was strongly suggested by some of the paranormal evidence. And yet the physiological facts remained, and told strongly against the hypothesis. How could these two sets of information be reconciled?

It seemed fairly clear to me that they could not. The only conclusion possible was that our view of reality must, as Arnold Toynbee has proposed, be defective at the most fundamental level. This conviction tended to grow as time went on, and I came to see this defect of vision expressing itself in a number of hoary antinomies: mind versus matter and free will versus determinism for example. Quite frequently some eminent contemporary philosopher would pronounce one of these venerable conundrums to have no real existence. I could only reply that they were real for me. John Beloff, in his recent book *The Existence of Mind*, has made it clear that one of these controversies at least is still very much alive.

As time went on I increasingly began to think of solving (in some sense) this central conundrum as my goal in life. I was not so immodest as to suppose I might do this intellectually. Bertrand Russell confesses in his autobiography that when he first started to study philosophy he had been impelled by the hope of finding answers to the great fundamental questions. An attempt by me to succeed where Russell had failed would not merely be futile, it would be ludicrous. In any case, so far as I could gather, contemporary philosophy had given up the attempt to solve such problems. Was there another way to try to answer what Aldous Huxley has called the cosmic intelligence test?

Dimly I saw that what was needed was a comprehensive approach, one making use not merely of the intellect but the whole being. This approach, I felt, must be through art.

Here I was deeply influenced by the poetic theory of Robert Graves. Graves' poetry had long been of the greatest importance to me, so it was natural that I should turn to him for an account of how poetry comes to be written. He compares a poem to the pearl which an oyster secretes in response to a particle of grit. The poet is obsessed by a particular emotional problem, and eventually this obsession reaches such a pitch that it induces the 'poetic trance' out of which a poem is born.

I was pretty sure I could never be a poet, but I felt that Graves' account could be extended to cover the writing of fiction. I had long wanted to write novels, and had started several that invariably bogged down after a few chapters. Now I began to think about writing as a possible way of achieving insight, self-integration. Could I hope, by a lifetime's work, to feel my way through ('by God and hope and hopelessness') to at least a measure of wisdom? (Robert Frost said: 'A poem begins in delight and ends in wisdom.')

Immediately after I qualified in medicine I started a new novel. It petered out after a couple of chapters as usual, but nevertheless I was pleasantly surprised by what seemed to me the quite reasonable quality of what I had written. A year or two later, for a variety of reasons, we went to live in Pari's home town, Tehran, where I took a teaching job at a newly set-up university. Almost as soon as I arrived I began a new novel, and within six weeks I had completed the first draft. This was an experience which I can only compare with falling in love. It was not difficult to believe that if I could return repeatedly to this state of exhilaration I should indeed achieve something like enlightenment. So for a year or more after completing my novel I went on trying to work the oracle again—fruitlessly, for my second novel would not get started. This was depressing enough; but worse, a little reflection on the lives of well-known writers showed that few of them, however prolific, gave much outward sign of having achieved self-integration. If enlightenment was my aim I should probably achieve it better as a farmer or a sailor than as a writer.

After two years in Tehran we came to London, and it was soon after this that I heard of transcendental meditation. It came at just the right time, for I was now in a condition of what I can only describe as spiritual aridity. On the face of it this was surprising, for our life was going well; I was doing reasonably congenial and well-paid work as a medical journalist, while Pari had taken up painting and sculpture, which she had always longed to do. But inwardly I felt life to be unbearably flat. The flatness showed itself in moods of depression and long hours of pen-sucking while I laboriously composed a few pages that next day went into the waste-paper basket.

An inability to write was not the whole trouble, however; indeed, it was as much a symptom as a cause. Looking back, I saw my life as rather like a narrative in verse written by a poet whose real talent was for *haiku*. There were peaks of intense experience separated by valleys of depression and wide plains of tedium. The peaks were mostly events which could hardly be repeated to order—falling in love, writing well; but there was one situation—travelling on foot through mountains—which seemed to be a fairly reliable inducer of such experiences. But even that was for the time being out of reach, and I felt the deprivation keenly. London was stifling after the sense of liberation, of expansion and freedom, which I had experienced in the vastness of the Persian landscape and sky. I know of nowhere in Europe that can match Persia for this ability to confer enlargement on the spirit. Spain, perhaps, comes nearest to it; but then, as the Spaniards say, Europe begins at the Pyrenees. The Persian deserts and mountains are magnificent, all shifting lights and variegated colours—pink, yellow, red, orange, purple; but what gives Persia its extraordinary evocativeness is not only its emptiness; paradoxically it is also its long association with man and his civilizations. Time in Persia is visibly a fourth dimension, and here the tomb of an emperor who died two and a half millenia ago, there the crumbling ruins of a caravanserai abandoned when the camel yielded to the motor car, afford the traveller an agreeable sense of melancholy.

One sees strange sights in Persia. I think of a Haji Firuz (a sort of New Year clown, traditionally black-faced and dressed in red) perched high in a tree beside the road in the middle of nowhere, singing and playing on a tambourine; and of an enormous grey bird (a dodo? a pterodactyl?) standing in the desert with its back to a wayside 'coffee house', ignoring, and ignored by, everyone. I cannot explain why this last scene is invested for me with a haunting quality of almost metaphysical significance. But, having lived in Persia, I find it easier to understand why the Sufis developed their habit of combining esoteric instruction with humour, that finds expression in some of the tales of Rumi's *Masnavi* as well as in innumerable popular jokes, such as those attributed to the immortal Mullah Nasrudin.

Before I returned to England I made an unforgettable solitary journey, mainly on foot, to the Castle of the Assassins in Alamut and thence northwards, over the high passes of the Alborz range and down through the dense rain-forests of the northern slopes to the Caspian shore. I had earlier done a certain amount of rather similar travelling in Greece, but I have seldom known happiness of the intensity that I experienced in the Alborz. What causes such happiness? Is it the altitude? Does it come in spite of physical fatigue, or because of it? I do not know; but certainly there is a connection between mountains and ecstasy. (Eric Newby gives an interesting account of such an experience in his *A Short Walk through the Hindu Kush*.) One of the most important spurs to undertaking travel of this kind is, I am sure, the knowledge—whether fully conscious or not does not matter—that it can give rise to these unusually intense experiences. My own minute tastes of this have led me to believe that the extraordinary qualities of spirit which come so clearly through the writings of many great mountaineers and travellers—Robert Byron, Wilfrid Thesiger, Freya Stark, for example—are in part due to their exposure to such influences. For happiness of this kind is not a merely passive experience; it is a transforming activity, which inevitably changes the personality to some degree.

The American psychologist Abraham Maslow has written a great deal about the value of such 'peak experiences'. (They are not, of course, confined to mountain tops; but the pun is, I am sure, more than accidental.) After my return to London I realized that at least occasional experience of happiness of this quality was as essential to me as air. It so far transcended everything else that I would willingly have confined my living to a succession of these moments; yet my life was going in the wrong direction, becoming channelled into ways that made the occurrence of such moments more and more unlikely. I knew that I was wasting time that was infinitely precious, but I did not know what else to do. One could go to a village in Crete or Spain and live on very little, but not on nothing at all. Had I been single I might well have given up my job and gone off to Nepal for a time. As it was, I waited.

Nevertheless it was something to know, however late, what it was that one wanted, even if it was the impossible. For obviously it was impossible to live all one's days in ecstasy. Joy by its very nature is transitory, as almost every poet down the ages has told us. I never for a moment questioned this evident truth.

Yet it seems I was wrong.

By now I had in my possession pretty well all the pieces of the puzzle; all I had to do was to fit them together. But of course, like everyone else in countless earlier generations, I was trying to assemble them the wrong way round.

In 1967 the late lamented BBC Third Programme broadcast two talks by J. M. Cohen. The first described the fourteen years which Cohen spent as a follower of Ouspensky, while the second dealt with his discovery of transcendental meditation. I had previously read Cohen's study of Robert Graves and also knew him as a translator of Spanish verse, so I was naturally interested in the story of his own development and its outcome. Nevertheless, my long-standing prejudice against esotericism was still strong, and I do not think that I should have done anything practical about transcendental meditation were it not for a single remark of Cohen's. This meditation, he said, was meant for everyone.

For me this was the essential point. I wrote to Cohen, asking how Pari and I could learn to meditate. A week or two later we were attending an introductory talk in the Caxton Hall.

On that first evening I took in very little of what was said. My own previous interest in the subject was blocking my understanding; automatically I was trying to fit what I heard into my established conceptual scheme. One thing, however, would not fit: the claim that transcendental meditation was easy. Every book I had ever read had insisted on the immense difficulty of meditation. How could it possibly be easy?

What decided me to learn the meditation was not so much what was said as the quality of the two speakers. One of them in particular gave such an impression of vitality and happiness that I could not doubt that he was speaking the truth.

The next weekend saw Pari and me, equipped with fruit, flowers, and a new white handkerchief each, ringing the bell of a flat in Richmond and feeling remarkably foolish. I almost turned tail at the last moment, but was sustained by a conviction that it was now or never. My years of searching had brought me to the brink of practical experiment; I simply had to find out.

There is an unfortunate tendency for writers on esoteric subjects to lead the eager reader on to a certain point and then stop, hinting darkly at secrets which cannot be revealed. This trick is irritating the first few times one meets it, but later one recognizes it as simply a device for concealing the author's sad lack of any secret. I hope I shall not be accused of practising the same deception when I say that I shall not be describing either the technique of the meditation itself or my own experiences during meditation. There are good reasons for this. To give details of either aspect of transcendental meditation would not only be of no help, but would actually be a disservice to anyone who decided to experiment for himself. For although the meditation is the same for everyone, it has to be given individually. This is because to 'transcend' necessarily means to move along a new and hitherto unexplored dimension of the mind; and although the process is natural and effortless, the experiences are so unfamiliar that a guide in the early stages is quite essential. Not that the experiences are invariably dramatic or startling—indeed, they may well be just the reverse, in which case it is their 'ordinariness' that will need to be explained!

I myself, being by temperament always inclined to look for knowledge in books, found this aspect of transcendental meditation somewhat irritating at first; but experience of the meditation, and of teaching it to others, has convinced me that in this area books would be quite useless. In this respect, I am sure, the ancient tradition of India is wholly in the right: any teaching of value must be passed on orally; there is simply no other way.

On the other hand, it is possible to say something about the meditation's practical effects. In my case a very early effect—it appeared within a week or so of my starting to meditate—was that I became much less tired. Whereas before I had always arrived home in the evening worn out, now I felt perfectly fresh. At first I could not believe that this was anything but a temporary phenomenon probably quite unconnected with meditation, but it continued and even increased.

The most remarkable change, however, was a new clarity of mind. It was as if a chatter of voices inside my head had suddenly fallen silent. I had never before been aware of this turmoil of irrelevant futile thoughts, that had revealed themselves now only by their cessation, rather as the Japanese are said to employ caged crickets as 'negative watchdogs' that sound an alarm by falling silent. It will be objected, I suppose, that this was an effect of suggestion; but certainly I had not been led to expect anything of the kind.[1]

Other effects of transcendental meditation appeared in these early days. Several people who did not know I was meditating spontaneously remarked that I looked better. And at home the effects were striking: Pari and I grew closer than we had ever been; quarrels, if they occurred, blew over in half the time they had lasted previously. The children behaved better because we were more patient.

Yet although I was now pretty sure that transcendental meditation produced practical effects, I still was only half-satisfied. My suspicions that meditation was a form of self-hypnosis were, if anything, stronger than before; I had no real insight into what I was doing. I knew Maharishi had written a book, but I did not read it—the truth is that I feared I might be disappointed.

Three months after I started to meditate a residential course was held in Wales. The idea was to allow longer time for

[1] Indeed, as is the practice when one learns to meditate, I had not been told what to expect at all. And in fact the first couple of times I meditated nothing did happen. This almost confirmed my worst fears. The reason, however, was that my preconceptions about the nature of meditation were interfering with the practice; instead of *letting* things happen I was trying to force them. When I returned to my teacher next day the fault was put right, and immediately I found that definite effects began to occur.

meditation; also, Maharishi himself was to conduct it. Pari and I decided to attend.

From the beginning we enjoyed the course much more than we expected. My fears of being associated with cranks were by no means allayed yet, but in fact we were both greatly impressed by many of the meditators we met. But Maharishi himself was at first sight a disappointment. I do not quite know what I expected a great spiritual teacher to be like, but certainly I did not expect this tiny figure, constantly bubbling over with laughter. He was disconcerting; he made me think of a blob of mercury, bright and mobile, unpredictable, impossible to seize. The only thing I was sure of was that he was totally unlike anyone I had ever met. We soon realized, however, that all these superficial impressions were beside the point. It was contrary to all my instincts and habits of mind to admit such a thing, but I saw that Maharishi was so original a teacher that my normal standards of judgement were quite inappropriate. By the time he left, both Pari and I knew that he had changed our lives beyond recall. I do not mean that we were swept away by some great flood of emotion; we simply recognized that we had crossed a watershed.

Throughout the succeeding years I have become more and more convinced that Maharishi's coming out into the world with his system of meditation is by far the most important event of our time. This seems—and is—a large claim, but I believe it can be justified. For I think that Maharishi's teaching offers us the possibility of achieving something which to many people today seems an utter impossibility: I mean a restoration of a lost wholeness in our view of ourselves and the world.

I make no apology for saying that the quest for wholeness (surely it is significant that the word is cognate with 'holiness'?) is a quest for religion, in the widest sense of the word. This was the belief of one of the few real sages of modern times, C. G. Jung, who held that the fundamental cause of most neurosis, especially during middle life and later, was a lack of religion, of a sense of purpose and security in an indifferent or hostile universe.

The cause of the downfall of religion has of course been largely the growth of science. It is sometimes claimed that science and religion are not really incompatible; but too often reconciliation between them is achieved only at the cost of sacrificing the vitality of both parties; there is little to be gained from a meeting between two ghosts. At the present time a full-blooded scientific view of the world seems to leave little room for compromise. Jacques Monod, the Nobel prizewinner, has unhesitatingly affirmed that life is an accident and therefore, presumably, meaningless. What room can such a belief leave for any religion worth the name?

Yet, for whatever reasons, many people continue to long for a reconciliation. The extraordinary success of Teilhard de Chardin's writings is evidence of the intensity of this longing. Nevertheless, the current is still flowing strongly the other way. Put the ultimate questions about the purpose of life to a scientist and you will almost certainly get at best a confession of ignorance and at worst an assertion that all such questions are meaningless. And if science fails us, where are we to turn? To philosophy? But philosophy is scarcely in better case than religion. From being, as it was for Plato, the summit of human activity, it has degenerated to what A. J. Ayer has called 'talk about talk'. In other words, modern philosophers do not seriously try to tell us what the world is like, but only give rules for thinking about the findings of science. Philosophy, like science, does not seek to offer answers to the ultimate questions.

And if, in despair, one turns back to religion, what does one find? Often enough one is met by a confession of ignorance even here. One sign of religion's growing loss of self-confidence is the trend it increasingly shows towards this worldliness; Christianity is becoming little more than social work, and in some quarters Jesus of Nazareth seems to be regarded as a forerunner of Che Guevara. But a religion without a firm theology or eschatology has abandoned all claim to be taken seriously.

One is sometimes told that the answer lies in 'faith'. But what is faith? The cynics call it believing in what you know to be untrue. That may be a little harsh; but perhaps 'a willing suspension of disbelief' might be a fair definition. Faith is usually regarded as a virtue; I can never quite see why. To try to force oneself into an unwarranted belief seems to me an act of despair.

31

The position I myself start from is that the ultimate questions are indeed as valid today as they ever were. The attempt to ignore them seems to me arrogant and philistine, and to be explicable only as the expression of a curious temporary aberration of the human mind. I believe that the answering of them is, for each of us, our true purpose in life, and that we cannot be satisfied until we have done so. And of all the great questions that confront us, the most fundamental is that posed long ago by Plotinus: '*Who are we?*' In the last analysis, all knowledge depends upon *self*-knowledge; that will be my theme throughout this book. My hope is that I may succeed in conveying, however inadequately, something of the scope and importance of Maharishi's teaching.

It scarcely needs to be said that I am indebted beyond words to Maharishi himself, not only for the meditation itself, but also for many hours and days of discussion and immensely patient answering of questions. I am also most grateful to the many meditators who have helped me by discussion, advice, and encouragement; I am specially grateful to Dr Vernon Katz, whose expert knowledge of Indian philosophy has been invaluable. However, at the cost of repetition let me stress once more that this book represents, not a final statement, but rather a report of work in progress; and all the errors which it doubtless contains must be laid squarely at my own door.

# SEVEN STATES OF CONSCIOUSNESS

# CHAPTER I

## *Finding the Right Question*

IT HAS OFTEN been said that to ask the right question is already to be half way to the answer. I have described how my reflections and reading had led me to conclude that there must be some basic flaw in our perception of reality, but I still had not found precisely the right way of expressing the difficulty. Something was wrong with our view of the world, but what?

Curiously, it was not until I had been listening to Maharishi on and off and reading his books for about eighteen months that I suddenly realized that he had repeatedly both posed and answered the one central question which was the clue to the whole problem. 'Unless I know who I am,' he asks, 'how can I know anything at all?'

This is essentially the question asked by Plotinus: '*Who are we?*' On the answer we give to this most fundamental of all riddles depends everything we think and do. What is at issue is really the nature of the self. Is it the body? Is it the conglomeration of thoughts, desires, and emotions that seem to constitute the mind? Or is it something else?

The modern formulation of Plotinus' question is the 'mind-body problem'. Until recently in the West (and, indeed, in most societies of which we have knowledge), people generally assumed that man has both a body and a soul; the soul governs the body but can—as happens at death—be separated from it. An intellectual version of this almost universal primitive belief was put forward by Plato, whose philosophy is indeed saturated with the notion of psycho-physical dualism.

A different view was adopted by Aristotle, who, in his treatise *On the Soul*, held that all souls are forms or patterns of living bodies; and for the most part Aristotle seems ready to accept the natural conclusion that there is no personal immortality.

For the first millennium of the Christian era the Platonic

35

doctrine held sway in the West, but in the thirteenth century St Thomas Aquinas, perhaps rather surprisingly, rejected it in favour of Aristotle's biological theory. (The reason may have been his abhorrence of Albigensianism, which the Platonic theory might seem to support.) At the Renaissance there was a reversion to the Platonic view, which was given a detailed formulation by Descartes. Somewhat paradoxically, Descartes was for the most part an extreme mechanist (he went so far as to localize the point of interaction between soul and body to the pineal gland), and his influence was paramount in scientific thinking until modern times.

In this century, however, there has once more been a swing from Platonism back towards Aristotelianism, which seems to some philosophers and many scientists to be more in keeping with recent discoveries in biology. The most important criticism of the Cartesian answer to the mind-body problem has come from Gilbert Ryle, with his well-known gibe at the 'ghost in the machine'. Ryle holds that the whole problem has arisen as the result of faulty thinking, and that if once we set this right the concept of mind will vanish away like a puff of smoke. Mind, he says, is a 'category mistake'. If we look for the mind we are like a foreigner who, watching a game of cricket, complains that although he can see the players, bats, wickets, ball, and so on, he cannot see the team spirit of which he has heard so much.

Ryle's views agree quite closely with those of the Behaviourist school in psychology (though Ryle himself denies that he is a behaviourist). A rather similar approach characterizes probably most people who are working today on the brain itself. Brain researchers usually seem to lean towards the view that brain states and mental states are different aspects of the same thing. In other words, if I see an apple certain electrochemical events (which cannot yet be described in detail) occur in my brain, and these events have, in addition to their physical character, another character by virtue of which I recognize them as the experience 'seeing an apple'. A number of modern philosophers, especially in Australia, have worked on the theoretical implications of the 'identity thesis', as this approach is called.

It is easy to see why most neurophysiologists favour some version of the identity thesis. Ever since the first man got drunk on fermented grape juice or lost his wits as the result of a blow from a club in battle, it must have been obvious that chemical and physical agents could profoundly modify personality. But modern studies of the brain have extended this knowledge widely and deeply; we now know that almost every aspect of our mental and emotional life can be altered by surgery, drugs, or electrical stimulation. Technology has short-circuited centuries of philosophical speculation.

Of course it is important not to exaggerate all this. As I have said, a good deal was already known to the ancients, and modern science has, in general, only refined this knowledge. True, science promises (or threatens) more far-reaching possibilities—transfer of memories from one individual to another, for example—but these developments are still in the domain of science fiction. Nevertheless, the knowledge we already possess is enough to constitute, in many people's eyes, a threat to individual integrity. If so much of our personality can, even if only in principle, be manipulated, what is left? Our hopes, our fears, our loves, our memories, our thoughts— none seem any longer fully our own.

A different sort of threat seems to be posed by computers. Already machines can exceed the human brain in certain capacities. What does the future hold? Will man, a sort of inferior computer on legs, be reduced to a mere acolyte attending on a world of machines that has no further need of him?

These remarks will, I hope, go to show that the mind-body problem is no dry-as-dust topic without practical relevance, but on the contrary vitally affects politics, medicine, sociology, jurisprudence, and above all religion. How we conceive of ourselves is crucial to the kind of world we build. Many of our present ills are, I believe, consequent on a loss of confidence in ourselves engendered by the discoveries of science from Copernicus through Darwin into modern times. For science has displaced, first man's world, then man himself, from the special position they once seemed to hold in the universe. And the impact of neurophysiology, which is only now beginning to be felt, is likely to be far greater than that of any scientific discovery that has gone before.

The older view of man seemed to afford him a place in the total scheme of things—even, sometimes, a kinship with the gods. That place has come to seem less and less secure with each successive intellectual revolution, until man, far from thinking of himself as fashioned in the image of God, now regards himself as the accidental by-product of an impersonal universe in which his joy and sorrow, success and failure, have no more meaning than do the patterns of clouds or the ripples on a lake. Despair at this loss of meaning appears to be at the root of much of the contemporary interest in the 'occult', which seems to offer a refuge from the oppressive weight of scientific orthodoxy.

To adopt a wilful obscurantism would, of course, be futile. If scientific materialism is true we must make the best of it; no purpose will be served by a flight into irrationalism. But before we resign ourselves to what may seem a bleak prospect, let us at least make sure that we are not substituting one mythology for another. Are we quite sure that our present somewhat austere concept of man's nature is any truer than the one we had before?

In thinking about this problem I have usually found that I got more help from scientists themselves than I did from philosophers. This may sound surprising; but perhaps the explanation is that the working scientist—especially the neurophysiologist —who stops to think about the fundamentals of his subject is bound to be brought up against the problem directly, whereas the philosopher in his study can afford a certain degree of Olympian detachment which may or may net be helpful. At all events, in this chapter I shall be looking in some detail at ideas which have preoccupied some of the leading scientists of our time. And I should like to start by quoting some attempts simply to state the problem without solving it.

Sir Charles Sherrington has been described, with reason, as the father of modern neurophysiology. In his classic *Man on his Nature* (Cambridge University Press, 1940) Sherrington confessed himself frankly baffled by the problem of how mind acted on matter and vice versa. 'Mind,' he wrote, 'for anything perception can compass, goes therefore in our spatial world more ghostly than a ghost. Invincible, intangible, it is a thing not even of outline; it is not a "thing". It remains without sensual confirmation and remains without it for ever.' (p. 357.)

Notice that Sherrington, unlike a number of modern philosophers, does not try to explain the problem away. He sees it as cardinal to our understanding of the world and ourselves—this is the whole theme of his book—but he cannot see how it could possibly be resolved.

In 1966 an international congress of brain researchers was held (at the Vatican, curiously) to discuss this topic. No conclusion was reached, but the report of the participants' deliberations—*Brain and Conscious Experience* (Springer-Verlag), edited by J. C. Eccles, himself one of the world's leading neurophysiologists and proponent of a view of the brain as a mechanism designed to amplify the impulses of a non-physical mind—makes most fascinating reading. It contains some clear and frank admissions of perplexity. Wilder Penfield, for example, remarked in the course of his paper: 'If we are good scientists, we cannot claim that science has already explained the mind nor that it has thrown any light on man's long continued effort to understand his God. I wonder if it ever will.' (*BCE*, p. 218.)

Similar passages could be quoted from the writings of many modern scientists. I will content myself with only one more— an especially explicit statement of the problem by a leading biologist, C. H. Waddington: 'We confront, in the problem of self-awareness, a basic mystery which lies at the heart of our whole life. . . . We can explain to ourselves some of the mechanisms by which, for instance, light waves emitted from an object are focused on our retina, and there cause electrical disturbances which travel into and around our brains. But the most essential step in the whole process is that these events cause us to be aware of something; and so long as we have not the faintest idea what this awareness means, and *cannot envisage any way in which the phenomenon of awareness could be expressed in terms of anything else*, the act of perception and the whole observable world which depends on it, contains an inescapable element of mysteriousness. . . . Since the nature of self-awareness completely resists our understanding, the natural philosophy of biology cannot but bring us face to face with the conclusion that, however much we may understand certain aspects of the world, *the very fact of existence as we know it in our experience is essentially a mystery.*' (*The Nature of Life*, Allen & Unwin, 1961, pp. 119–20. My italics.)

The heart of the problem lies in the words which I have italicized. It is because we are *aware* that we know there is a world at all. To know anything about *awareness* seems to demand an impossible reflexive act—like trying to see your own eye. There is an extraordinary anticipation of this in the Upanishads, where the question is posed: '*How can the knower be known?*' And this question finds a modern echo in Kurt Gödel's famous theorem: in every logical system (provided it is sufficiently comprehensive to include the axioms of arithmetic) there exist statements which are meaningful but which can neither be proved nor disproved. In other words, such a system can never prove its own truth; if it tries to do so it is like a man trying to lift himself up by his shoe laces.

Here, then, we have the ultimate question, upon which all other questions depend. All our much-vaunted scientific knowledge is without a foundation unless we know ourselves, unless we have some focus, some 'still point of the turning world' to which everything can be related. And this is not merely an intellectual problem, of interest only to philosophers and philosophically minded scientists; it is of the greatest possible importance to everyone. Solving it means, in fact, reorganizing one's 'self' so that the answer to the question: 'Who am I?' expresses itself in every phase of existence. This, I am sure, was the real meaning of the Socratic injunction 'know thyself'. It was not an intellectual—or even psychological—understanding that Socrates was interested in; he was speaking of what the great Eastern religions have termed 'enlightenment'.

The difference between an intellectual understanding of the truth and an actual living of it will, I hope, emerge more clearly later in the book. At present I am concerned to take the intellectual approach as far as it will go, partly with the aim of showing in what respects it falls short. I should therefore like to turn to the views of Erwin Schrödinger.

Schrödinger was, of course, one of the most brilliant of modern physicists, Professor of Physics at the University of

Vienna and discoverer of wave mechanics. He started out as a philosopher, becoming deflected into physics only later; and he retained his interest in philosophy to the end of his life. He was thus in an unusually favourable position to assess the implications of science for our understanding of ourselves in the world. He discussed these questions in several books; his mature conclusions are set forth in *Mind and Matter* (Cambridge University Press, 1958).

Schrödinger's solution to the problem of mind is simple but radical; he denies the validity of the separation of subject and object. The idea that there are as many separate egos as there are bodies and that each ego perceives its own version of the (objective) world is, he says, a mistake.

The conventional view is something like this: on the one hand there is the object—an apple, say—and on the other there is the subject, the perceiver. But this idea leads to all sorts of difficulties: does the apple 'really' have the properties of being red, smooth, sweet-smelling, and so on, or are these qualities in some way added on by the mind—and if so, what is the real nature of the apple?

All such questions, Schrödinger thinks, stem from the fundamental error of separating subject and object. In reality there is no separation, only a seeming separation which mind induces for the purpose of simplification. In truth mind has given rise to everything. 'Mind has created the objective outside world of the natural philosopher out of its own stuff. Mind could not cope with this gigantic task otherwise than by the simplifying device of excluding itself—withdrawing from its own creation.' (*MM*, p. 131.) But this device is concealed in two ways. 'First, my own body (to which my mental activity is so very directly and intimately linked) forms part of the object (the real world around me) that I construct out of my sensations, perceptions, and memories. Secondly, the bodies of other people form part of this objective world. Now I have very good reasons for believing that these other bodies are also linked up with, or are, as it were, the seats of spheres of consciousness. I can have no reasonable doubt about the existence or some kind of actualness of these foreign spheres of consciousness, yet I have absolutely no direct subjective access to any of them. Hence I am inclined to take them as something objective, as forming part of the real world around me. Moreover, since there is no distinction between myself and others, but on the contrary full symmetry for all intents and purposes, I conclude that I myself also form part of this real material world around me. I so to speak put my own sentient self (which had constructed this world as a mental product) back into it—with the pandemonium of disastrous logical consequences that flow from the aforesaid chain of faulty conclusions.' (*MM*, pp. 127–8.)

The most serious of the antinomies that flow from this error are, first, the absence of colour and sound, hot and cold, from our world model (since these are our immediate sensations, we have abstracted them from the model along with our 'mental person'), and secondly, the free will paradox.

This is the point which had specially puzzled Sherrington (from whom Schrödinger quotes extensively). How can an immaterial mind act on a material body? For Schrödinger the answer lies in the same artificial separation of subject and object. The material world has been constructed at the price of removing mind from it; mind therefore obviously cannot act on the world. Notice that this paradox cannot be 'got round'. 'The impasse *is* an impasse. Are we not thus the doers of our deeds? Yet we feel responsible for them, we are punished or praised for them, as the case may be. It is a horrible antinomy. I maintain that it cannot be solved on the level of present-day science which is still entirely engulfed in the "exclusion principle"—without knowing it—hence the antinomy.' (*MM*, pp. 131–2.)

What Schrödinger is saying in all this is that the personality is not localized 'in' the head, as we tend unconsciously to assume. 'It is very difficult for us to take stock of the fact that the localization of the personality, of the conscious mind, inside the body is only symbolic, just an aid for practical use.' (*MM*, p. 133.)

Where, then, are we to localize the mind, if not in the body? The answer is that we are not to localize it at all. 'Subject and object are only one. . . . The reason why our sentient, percipient, and thinking ego is met nowhere within our scientific world picture can easily be indicated in seven words: because it is itself that world picture. It is identical with the whole and therefore cannot be contained in it as part of it.' (*MM*, p. 137.)

The obvious difficulty with this suggestion is that there *appear* to be a great many separate egos. What is the explanation?

One possibility would be to say that there are really as many universes as egos; this would amount to Leibniz's monadology, which there seems no good reason to accept. The alternative is to conclude that there is only *one* mind. This is of course the message of the Upanishads as well as of the majority of mystics throughout the ages, though such support will for most scientifically-minded people be an added reason why the idea should be rejected. Schrödinger, however, is emphatic that it is precisely at this point that our thinking needs to be amended, though he is careful to point out that we do not wish to lose the logical precision of our scientific thought that has achieved so much.

Schrödinger does not claim to have completely assimilated the Eastern notion of oneness of mind into Western scientific thought, but in a remarkable passage he hints at the kind of readjustment in our thinking that will be needed.

'Mind is by its very nature a *singulare tantum*. I should say: the over-all number of minds is just one. I venture to call it indestructible since it has a peculiar time-table, namely mind is always *now*. There is really no before and after for mind. There is only a now that includes memories and expectations. But I grant that our language is not adequate to express this, and I also grant, should anyone wish to state it, that I am now talking religion, not science—a religion, however, not opposed to science, but supported by what disinterested scientific research has brought to the fore.' (*MM*, p. 145.)

Schrödinger has seen clearly where his ideas are leading. Science and religion are *not* ultimately in opposition; the parallel lines do meet at infinity. Science, like every other human activity, depends on the mind. On what does the mind depend? The answer to this question is, in the broadest sense, 'religious'.

# CHAPTER II

## *Pure Awareness*

THERE IS ONE important objection to Schrödinger's hypothesis of oneness of mind which so far I have not considered. I think that it is worth looking at in some detail, because it will lead on to an important idea with far-reaching implications.

The objection is this: surely the physiological evidence rules out the notion of oneness of mind at the outset? The findings of modern brain research seem to show conclusively that mind and brain, if not identical, are at least indissolubly linked together.

A particularly striking instance that might be adduced is that of the 'split-brain' patient. The brain has two hemispheres, whose functions differ; thus in right-handed people the left hemisphere is responsible for speech. (Each hemisphere largely controls the opposite side of the body.) The functions of the right hemisphere are poorly understood, but may be concerned with non-verbal thought.

Doctors in California have treated some patients with epilepsy by dividing the main nerve tracts that connect the two hemi-spheres, and the effects of these operations on mental functioning have been studied at the California Institute of Technology by Professor Roger Sperry and his team.

The effects of such seemingly drastic operations are sur-prisingly inconspicuous. Patients do not *feel* that they have been divided. However, refined methods of testing reveal some interesting effects. For example, a patient with a split brain can read aloud words which are shown to the left hemisphere but not those shown to the right; however, he can perceive quite well with the right hemisphere, for if an object is presented (by sight or touch) to the right hemisphere alone he can subsequently pick it out with the left hand from among a collection of objects. An even odder effect is produced if a picture of a nude is shown to the right hemisphere; the patient begins to chuckle but, because language is controlled from the left hemisphere, cannot explain why.

Findings such as these have led Sperry to say that 'surgical division of the brain also divides the mind into two separate realms of human consciousness'.

Sperry's views have been attacked on various grounds. For one thing, the patients concerned had abnormal brains to begin with, otherwise they would not have been operated upon. However, while their epilepsy may well have affected some of the results of the operations, the findings as a whole cannot be explained away on that score.

The late Sir Cyril Burt was unconvinced by Sperry's results, and emphasized the absence of any apparent subjective splitting of consciousness. To this objection Sperry would no doubt reply that consciousness is indeed split but that the right hemisphere, lacking access to speech, cannot make its awareness known except indirectly.

For my part, I should like to draw attention to a point which seems to me most important and insufficiently emphasized in most of the discussion; I mean the distinction between *mind* and *consciousness*. Most writers, including Schrödinger and Sperry, use these terms almost interchangeably, but from now on I shall have to distinguish them.

To do so I shall first need to bring out the idea that the nervous system is arranged *hierarchically*. That is, it is built up of a number of physiological and anatomical levels each of which is controlled by the one above at increasing levels of generality. (At the same time the traffic is two-way; the higher centres depend upon the lower ones for information, and if they fail to get it they often cease to operate properly.)

For example, an animal (or a human being) has a number of reflexes concerned with the maintenance of posture and with walking. These may be studied by making a cut through an appropriate part of the brain stem in such a way as functionally to isolate the brain stem. This 'decerebration' was first described in the cat by Sherrington in 1898; somewhat analogous effects are sometimes produced in man by injury or disease.

The 'decerebrate' animal can stand, and if one foot is stimulated all four limbs move to produce the actions of walking. All this activity is reflex, and is due to the arrangements of the connections within the spinal cord; it is not controlled by the 'will' of the animal, since the higher parts of the brain have been cut off from the rest by the operation. It is rather as if all communications between an army's headquarters and its outlying companies had been broken by an enemy; the officers and men would continue to carry out their functions but these would no longer be related to the needs of the army as a whole.

The spinal reflexes are fairly simple examples of automatic activity. The intact human nervous system can carry out highly skilled actions quite automatically, without the need of conscious direction. For instance, a man may drive a car through heavy traffic—a performance which requires an almost incredible degree of neuromuscular co-ordination—yet all the while be carrying out mathematical calculations in his head.

As one traces the arrangement of the nervous system upward, from the spinal cord through the brain stem and into the brain itself, one finds increasing levels of complexity. At the higher levels, but not at the lower, one encounters structures related to functions such as perception and emotion.

Now, it is possible to conceive of this hierarchical arrangement as continuing 'upward' into the realm we call mind. On this hypothesis, human personality will be something like a cone. The body and nervous system will be at the apex, while mind is the volume of the cone intermediate between the apex and the base.[1] *The base itself, which is to be thought of as infinite in extent, is consciousness.*

On this scheme, mind, although less 'material' than the body, does not cease to be part of the physical universe. Instead of being diametrically opposed to each other, mind and body lie on a continuum. It is between consciousness on the one hand and mind-body on the other that the real break occurs.

This scheme is tripartite rather than dualistic. One or another version of it has attracted many psychical researchers; and not only psychical researchers, as the philosopher H. H. Price has made clear: 'This tripartite division of human nature appears

---

[1] There is clearly room for a great deal of discussion and theorizing about the 'mind' region of the cone, but this would take me too far out of my way. See note on p. 89.

under various names in Neoplatonism, in some of the religious philosophies of the Far East, and in some Christian thinkers also. There are philosophical arguments in favour of it which have some weight; moreover, certain forms of mystical experience seem to support it.' (*Science and ESP*, ed. J. R. Smythies, Routledge & Kegan Paul, p. 41.)

For my purpose, the important point about the scheme is the position of consciousness. In the light of this idea we can, I think, evaluate Sperry's findings in his split-brain patients more accurately. Sperry has certainly demonstrated that *some* aspects of the *mind* appear to be divided. How far this goes—how deeply the 'mind-cone' is split—is, however, another question. But in any case, consciousness itself has not been affected, for *consciousness is not identical with the brain or the mind but is that which witnesses the changes which occur in brain and mind.*[1]

The concept of this 'third factor' receives interesting confirmation from some remarks of Wilder Penfield, the surgeon who has given such extraordinary accounts of the results he obtained by direct stimulation of the brains of conscious patients at operation. In such cases it is possible to elicit exceptionally vivid recollections of past experiences; the patient feels that he is actually reliving events of perhaps twenty years ago. Yet at the same time he is aware of his present surroundings—the operating theatre. And thirdly there is an overall awareness that recognizes both of these 'streams of consciousness' as going on at the same time. Here is Penfield striving, in the course of a discussion, to put this into words: 'If that is the case, that two streams of consciousness are being appreciated, then there is something more than the awareness of conscious experience: there is something that is capable of appreciating two conscious streams simultaneously and judging their relations to each other. There is something more that we come here to consider and cannot even name! There is something more that is able to see, and reflect, and compare such simple things as two streams of awareness. I am not expressing that very well, but I am sure you guess what I am driving at. There is something more than just the stream of awareness. . . . There is something beyond the stream of

[1] This idea is discussed in detail in Chapter VI.

conscious experience that we still are not either naming or identifying or understanding.' (*BCE*, p. 546.)

An analogy may help to make the idea clearer. There is a cinematographic trick whereby one sequence of pictures is photographed on one half of a film and a different sequence on the other half. When the whole film is projected on a screen one sees two films simultaneously. There is, however, only *one* screen. In the same way, there is only one over-arching awareness, upon which different parts of the brain may (in exceptional circumstances) project their several perceptions of the world.

If we extend this idea a little, we can suppose that, as Schrödinger and the Upanishads hold, all the *different* brains in the world also project their separate perceptions on the same screen.

No doubt it still seems a bizarre notion. However, I think it becomes easier to accept if one realizes that there is some empirical justification for it. If there really is a 'screen of awareness' apart from the nervous system, there ought to be some evidence of its existence, Now, we do in fact find precisely such evidence. There are a great many accounts which suggest that a state of 'pure awareness'—that is, just awareness itself, without the mind or body components—can occur.

This may well sound surprising. However, as W. T. Stace points out in his important book *Mysticism and Philosophy* (Macmillan, 1961), there is no doubt that many people do describe reaching a state of pure awareness. How could this come about?

Suppose, Stace says, that one first got rid of all sensations, then of all sensuous images, and finally of all abstract thought; what would be left of consciousness? 'One would suppose *a priori* that consciousness would then entirely lapse and one would fall asleep or become unconscious. But the introvertive mystics—thousands of them all over the world—unanimously assert that they have attained to this complete vacuum of particular mental contents, but that what then happens is quite different from a lapse to unconsciousness. On the contrary, what emerges is a state of *pure* consciousness—'pure' in the sense that it is not the consciousness *of* any empirical content. It has no content except itself. . . . The paradox is that there should be a positive experience which has no positive content—an experience which is both something and nothing.' (*MP*, p. 86.)

This experience has been reported by (among others) Tennyson and J. A. Symonds. Here is Tennyson: 'A kind of waking trance—this for lack of a better word—I have frequently had quite up from boyhood, when I have been quite alone. . . . All at once, as it were out of the intensity of the consciousness of individuality, individuality itself seemed to dissolve and fade away into boundless being, and this not a confused state but the clearest of the clear, the surest of the sure, utterly beyond words—where death was an almost laughable impossibility—the loss of personality (if so it were) seeming no extinction but the only true life.' (Quoted in VRE, p. 370n.)

And now Symonds: 'One reason why I disliked this kind of trance was that I could not describe it to myself. I cannot even now find words to render it intelligible. It consisted in a gradual but swiftly progressive obliteration of space, time, sensation, and the multifarious factors of experience which seem to qualify what we are pleased to call our Self. In proportion as these conditions of ordinary consciousness were subtracted, the sense of an underlying or essential consciousness acquired intensity. At last nothing remained but a pure, absolute, abstract Self. The universe became without form and void of content. But Self persisted, formidable in its vivid keenness. . . . The return to ordinary conditions of sentient existence began by my first recovering the power of touch, and then by the gradual though rapid influx of familiar impressions and diurnal interests. . . . I was thankful for this return from the abyss. . . . This trance recurred with diminishing frequency until I reached the age of twenty-eight. . . . Often have I asked myself with anguish, on waking from that formless state of denuded, keenly sentient being, which is the unreality—the trance of fiery, vacant, apprehensive, skeptical Self from which I issue, or these surrounding phenomena.' (Quoted in VRE, pp. 371–2.)

Descriptions such as these go to show that Schrödinger's view of the self as the canvas upon which mental events are depicted is more than a philosophical theory; it is in fact open to direct confirmation by experience.

The state of pure awareness is described in the Upanishads as the fourth state—'fourth' with reference to the three ordinary states of awareness: waking, dreaming, and dreamless sleep. (Admittedly some modern studies suggest that even in so-called dreamless sleep some form of mental activity does go on, but this does not affect the argument; the three states are clearly separable not only subjectively but physiologically.) These three 'relative' states are to be thought of as projected on, or reflected in, the underlying reality of the fourth state, pure awareness.

What this means is, I think, best explained by an analogy. Suppose you are in a cinema where a newsreel is being shown. In terms of the analogy this corresponds to the ordinary waking state. Next, suppose the newsreel is replaced by a surrealist film —*Un Chien Andalou*, perhaps; this will correspond to the dreaming state. Thirdly, suppose that the projector breaks down and the cinema is plunged into darkness. This corresponds to the state of dreamless sleep.

Notice that in none of these three sets of circumstances have you seen the actual screen, but only, at best, the images projected upon it. But now imagine that the projector is switched on without any film in it, so that white light falls on the screen. Only now do you see the screen itself. This state of affairs corresponds to the fourth state, pure awareness.

It is clear that the existence of psychological states like those described by Tennyson and Symonds (and, of course, many others), flatly contradicts the famous passage from Hume (Book I, Part iv, Section 6) which denies the existence of any self or ego and maintains that a person is 'nothing but a bundle or collection of different perceptions'. Yet perhaps the contradiction is more apparent than real. Hume was right in so far as he implied that the self cannot be found by introspection. There is, however, a different possibility, as I shall discuss in the next chapter.

# CHAPTER III

## *Practical Applications*

THE FOREGOING CHAPTERS have, I hope, established that a number of Western thinkers who have tried to make sense of the problem of consciousness have been led to a position closely resembling that of the Advaita Vedanta—that is, to the view that consciousness is one. Now, so long as this conclusion remains on the intellectual level it may well be a fascinating and satisfying subject of speculation, but it is unlikely to have many practical effects—and those that it does have may not always be favourable. It is curious that even Schrödinger, who was otherwise so acute, apparently failed to realize that the frequent Upanishadic references to 'knowledge' imply, not the sort of understanding which one might obtain from pondering on statements of the truth, but direct experience of it.

The case of Schopenhauer might be a warning against such a misunderstanding. Schopenhauer was, of all Western philosophers, the most deeply influenced by the Upanishads, to which he explicitly acknowledged his indebtedness; yet this intellectual knowledge seems not to have had much practical effect on his character, which, if Bertrand Russell's outline in his *History of Western Philosophy* is to be believed, remained crabbed, miserly and unattractive to the end of his life.

Of course, some theorists, like Stace, have realized that something more than merely intellectual understanding is presupposed by the Vedic texts, yet I think there is scarcely one who does not assume as an axiom that the way to experience is long and unremitting effort. Stace, for example, says 'there have to be great and continuous efforts at the control and discipline of the mind' (*MP*, p. 87). That this should be generally believed is hardly surprising, for nearly all the great 'mystics' of every religion, East and West, undoubtedly do imply that reaching pure awareness is a task of the utmost difficulty.

It is at this point that we come to what is, perhaps, Maharishi's most original and important insight. It is, indeed, so original that it is bound to appear violently unorthodox; and yet, like most ideas of genius, it is also utterly simple and even obvious once it is understood. (Whether it is really so novel as it appears is another question; Maharishi himself insists that it must have been found and lost again many times in the past.)

Maharishi's insight depends on a basic postulate of the Upanishads—and, indeed, of all interiorly oriented religions; that the state of pure awareness is, in its own nature, blissful. If this is true, Maharishi argues, *movement towards it must be natural*. It is to be reached, not by control, but by letting go; not by concentrating the mind, but by letting it expand.

That the state of pure awareness should be blissful may at first sight seem surprising, but I think it need not really be so. After all, what happens as one approaches this state is that one moves from a region of relative turmoil (the waking state) to one of supreme peace, and this is naturally experienced as bliss. It is rather like falling asleep when one is tired—except for the vitally important difference that in meditation awareness *increases* rather than decreases.

Admittedly, this is to put the matter too negatively. The happiness of the state of pure awareness is something entirely positive; indeed, as I shall discuss in Chapter XI, it can be argued that *all* happiness in the outer world is a reflection of the inner bliss of the Self. At present, however, it is simpler to keep the discussion on the level of experience; and movement 'inwards'. towards pure awareness, is regularly found by meditators to be accompanied by increasing happiness.

Thus the principle which underlies transcendental meditation is that one does not *try* to gain the state of pure awareness, but allows oneself to be drawn in that direction naturally. Bliss supplies the motive power that draws the attention inwards, as gravity draws matter towards the centre of the earth.

The attention is constantly searching for happiness. In cybernetic parlance, it is a scanning mechanism, looking for happiness in the external world through the senses. But since the external world is, as Heraclitus pointed out, in a constant state of flux, the happiness which the mind discovers there can never be permanent. The inner pure awareness is permanent happiness, however, and therefore if the attention is once pointed towards it no deviation will occur.

The passage of the attention from the superficial level of the objective world, through the various intermediate regions of the mind, to the innermost layer of all, the Self, is the process of 'transcending'. It is difficult to avoid using spatial metaphors to describe this, but they do no harm provided they are not pushed too far. The image which Maharishi often uses is that of diving. Ordinary thinking is like swimming on the surface of a pool; meditation is like diving into the depths.

Sherrington has a remarkable anticipation of this view of the mind as a pool. Our mind, he says, is constantly in motion; we pass from one conscious act to another. Suppose you are looking at an aeroplane when you hear a cry from the street below. Immediately a new situation is created. The cry is perceived as part of a 'mental complex' composed of something heard (the cry), place (the street), the time (now); the cry is identified as, say, a child's voice. Where, Sherrington asks, did all this come from?

'The physical sound in the ear was just a physical vibration. How did it generate this mental complex which seems suddenly to invade the mind full-fledged? . . . How was it produced? Out of what was it constructed? . . . Its beginnings are unreachable by our mind, though our mind is the only means which could reach them. There would seem therefore to be a grade or grades of mind which we do not experience, as well as the mind which is our mental experience . . .

'The transition from recognizable mind to unrecognizable seems gradual. The mind which we experience, if we try to extend our experience into the process of its making, seems to become almost at once unable to be experienced. It eludes us by becoming subconscious. It is as though our mind were a pool of which the movements on the surface only were what we experience. The mind which we experience, that is, which *is* our mental experience, seems to emerge from elements of mind which we do not experience.' (*Man on His Nature*, pp. 239–40.)

All analogies are, of course, subject to limitations. But the comparison of the mind to a pool is quite helpful in thinking about the process of 'transcending', which consists essentially in 'extending our experience' into the 'making' of our minds. In particular, it should help to make clear the meaning of two most important technical terms. If you refer to fig. 1, you will see that going deeper within the mind means moving in the direction of increasing '*subtlety*', while movement in the opposite direction, towards the surface, is towards increasing '*grossness*'. I shall have to use these terms frequently from now on, so I must try to make them clear.

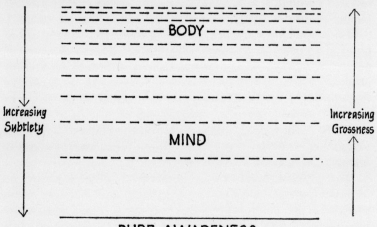

*Fig 1.*

The concept of 'subtlety' is used by Maharishi in a number of contexts. On the physical level, for example, the molecule is subtler than the crystal, the atom is subtler than the molecule, the sub-atomic particles are subtler than the atom, and so on. On the mental scale, one can similarly have subtler levels of thought, though these are not usually appreciated consciously. This is precisely Sherrington's point in the passage I quoted just now. Occasionally, however, one may be aware of a thought that flashes through the mind and is gone almost before one realizes it was there; this is an example of a 'subtle' thought. Notice that the idea of subtlety is not concerned with *meaning*; it is the quality and not the content of the thought that matters.

Meditation consists in appreciating thought at subtler and subtler levels, until eventually the subtlest level is 'transcended' and the experiencer is left alone with nothing to experience; this is the state of pure awareness.

Clearly one has to use some particular thought to experience in this way, and in practice this is the thought of a sound, or *mantra*.[1] In India it is believed that the choice of mantra is most important, because as one reaches subtler levels of the mind thought becomes vastly more 'powerful', in the same way that atomic forces are much more powerful than chemical ones.[2] I believe it was a recognition of the power of thought at these levels that prompted Jung's warnings about the dangers of uncontrolled 'irruptions of the unconscious'. According to Indian views—presumably based on experience—use of an incorrect thought could be ineffective or even destructive. A properly trained teacher is therefore essential.

Yet the teacher's only task is to give the meditator a right start. I cannot stress too often that the meditation, once its principle is understood, proceeds quite automatically. Nor—and this is most important—need the meditator be naturally calm or introspective; transcendental meditation is completely independent of psychological type, for it is based upon universals— the inherent tendency of all minds to search for happiness, and the inherently blissful nature of the inmost Self.

Once the attention has been turned in the correct direction it will inevitably tend inwards, because greater happiness lies there. And at each step reinforcement occurs, for as the 'depth of mind' intervening between the attention and its goal becomes less, the bliss of pure awareness becomes more and more apparent, like a light shining through fog.

Because transcendental meditation is a natural process, no special circumstances or preparations are needed to practise it;

[1] The underlying psychological theory (which has many parallels in the West) is that thought is a subtler version of sense perception. It follows that in principle one might transcend using any of the senses, but sound is apparently the easiest in practice and has been chosen by Maharishi for this reason.

[2] It is the sound, or vibrational, effects of the mantra to which I am referring here. It is interesting that a number of theories concerned with vibration have recently been put forward by people working on different scientific questions, including the formation of crystals and the development of embryos.

the meditator simply sits in any comfortable position, and the only prerequisite is a reasonably intact nervous system—that is, a nervous system which is capable of supporting thought.

Meditation is ordinarily practised twice a day for fifteen or twenty minutes on each occasion. During each meditation period several 'dives' occur; that is, the attention passes from superficial to deeper levels of thought and then frequently beyond, into the state of pure awareness. Every dive is followed by a return to the surface. The sequence of events can be represented diagrammatically (see fig. 2).

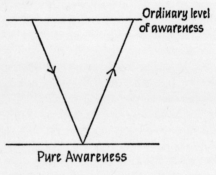

Fig 2.

During each full dive the attention necessarily traverses the full depth of the mind. In this way one becomes increasingly familiar with the subtler regions, and more able to make use of them. I shall return to this point in Chapter IX.

It may seem surprising that, if the state of pure awareness is indeed transcendental bliss, the attention ever returns to the ordinary state of awareness. What is it that calls the diver back to the surface? The answer to this question brings in a whole new aspect of transcendental meditation.

When Maharishi first came to the West he foretold that scientific studies would one day show that his technique of meditation produced definite results, and that these would consist in a reduction in body metabolism. This forecast has now been confirmed, and in the Appendix I have summarized the results obtained so far. Here I should like to say only that the principal effect is a fall in the metabolic rate (the rate at which the body burns up its fuel) to levels lower than those occurring in deep sleep. The meditator may appreciate this in terms of reduction in his rate and volume of breathing; in one study, a subject was breathing during meditation at a rate of only four breaths per minute (in place of the normal twelve or more) and these breaths were almost certainly very shallow. Such a person should be literally blue in the face from lack of oxygen, yet nothing of the sort occurs; the oxygen level in his blood remains normal, and there is no build-up of carbon dioxide.

It is important to understand that these changes are not the result of *controlling* the breathing. A number of recent studies have shown that conditioning can alter autonomic functions (blood pressure, heart rate, and so on) and the electrical activity of the brain, but in transcendental meditation all the physiological changes occur purely as by-products of the mental experience. To understand why this is so, consider what happens when one runs: blood pressure rises, heart rate increases, breathing becomes faster and deeper, and so on. These changes accompany, and reflect, the increased metabolic rate of the muscles. When one is walking the metabolic rate is lower; and when one is sitting quietly it is lower still. Now, the 'dive' of transcendental meditation represents the experiencing of 'subtler' regions of thought, and on the physiological level this corresponds to a reduction in metabolic rate. Thus, as the mind begins to experience finer mental activity, the body automatically follows. Indeed, unless the body does co-operate in this way, finer mental states will not be experienced.

Here is the explanation of the return to the surface after the dive. There is a limit to the length of time for which the body can sustain the reduced state of metabolism which accompanies the transcendental state. At first this time is short; later it lengthens somewhat, but always there comes a point when ordinary activity has to be resumed.

Yet that is not quite the whole story, for eventually pure awareness does become a permanent reality. I shall take up this theme again in the next chapter.

No doubt the idea of confirming the validity of a 'spiritual' practice by physiological research will be surprising and even shocking to some. Yet, to my mind, here is one of the most exciting things about transcendental meditation: it represents the long-awaited meeting point between science and religion. Since the eighteenth century at least, the twin rails of science and religion have been diverging wider and wider, leaving the unfortunate passengers in the train to jolt unhappily on over the sleepers. Today, probably, few people even hope for a reconciliation. Yet Maharishi serenely and confidently treats them as if they had never been separated, and there seems every chance that he is going to be vindicated by the results.

In Indian philosophy, of course, the Western idea of a rigid separation between mind and matter never took root, and physical methods (hatha yoga) have always been an important means of achieving union (yoga).[1]

The physiological studies of transcendental meditation are still in their infancy, of course. However, one conclusion is already possible. In the last chapter I discussed the notion of a fourth state of awareness in addition to the three ordinary states of waking, dreaming, and dreamless sleep. Since about 1962 it has been known that each of these 'relative' states can be distinguished on the basis of its physiological features. Thus in dreamless sleep the metabolic rate, heart rate, and blood pressure fall, while in dreaming they rise and the eyes move about rapidly. The experiments so far conducted on transcendental meditation make it clear that it produces a state which is physiologically as well as psychologically quite distinct from the waking, dreaming, and dreamless sleep states.

[1] This raises the whole question of the various 'systems' of yoga, of which hatha yoga is one. Its aim is to produce, by physical means, the state of the nervous system which is responsible for 'enlightenment'. Whether this can ever be done by purely physical means I do not know; but if it can, it requires many years of intense and possibly dangerous practice under the constant supervision of a fully competent master.

The understanding of yoga which is current in India today is that the various systems represent a ladder up which the aspirant is expected to progress in a regular manner. For Maharishi, on the other hand, they are more like the spokes of a wheel, of which transcendental meditation is the hub. By practising transcendental meditation one automatically improves not only the mind but also the body; hence there is thus no need for any other practice. Transcendental meditation, according to Maharishi, is the very heart and soul of yoga.

The state produced by meditation is, as I have said, characterized by deep physical relaxation, with a fall in the metabolic rate even more profound than that which occurs in deep sleep (although the subject remains alert). Now, a number of recent studies have strongly suggested that both dreaming and deep sleep are necessary to full mental and physical health. It is believed at present that deep sleep is necessary for repair of the body, dreaming for recuperation of the brain. At all events, people deprived of sleep for any length of time show severe mental and physical effects, while deprivation of dreaming has less dramatic, though measurable, effects. (Sleep deprivation has been used as a means of torture.) It seems entirely reasonable to suppose that the very profound rest which occurs during transcendental meditation is also necessary to the organism, and that lack of this rest is responsible for the accumulation of stress and, ultimately, much mental and physical ill-health.

This idea makes it possible to look at meditation in very simple terms. Forgetting all about the profounder questions, one can see it merely as a technique for providing much deeper rest than can be obtained even by sound sleep. The result of this deep rest is better functioning of the nervous system and hence enhanced clarity of the mind. In subsequent chapters I shall try to show that on this simple basis one can explain, clearly and comprehensively, the whole perplexing question of 'higher' states of consciousness.

So far as one can tell the physiological changes in transcendental meditation are unique. By that I mean that they distinguish the effects of this meditation from those of other methods and practices, with one possible exception which I shall discuss in a moment. In particular, they show that transcendental meditation is not, as is sometimes alleged, self-hypnosis. The physiological changes in hypnosis show wide variations, but these appear to be related to the type of suggestion which has been given. Attempts to lower the metabolic rate by means of suggested deep relaxation have not succeeded. In the hypnotic trance itself there are, it appears, no characteristic physiological changes at all, and indeed this has led some psychologists to deny the very existence of hypnosis, which they assert to be 'role playing'. As Tart points out, there is no agreed definition of 'trance'. (*Altered States of Consciousness*, Wiley, p. 3.)

(Of course, transcendental meditation differs from hypnosis in a number of other ways as well; for example, the technique bears no resemblance to any method of hypnotic induction. Hypnosis is notoriously hard to define, but at least one can say that suggestion plays a large part in it. In transcendental meditation, on the other hand, suggestion plays no part at all.)

One study of the electrical activity of the brain (electro-encephalogram) during Zen meditation has yielded results which somewhat resemble those found in people practising transcendental meditation. This is the possible exception which I mentioned just now. However, there is a most important difference; in the case of Zen meditation, the really unusual features were found in monks with over twenty years' experience of meditation, whereas the same features appeared in people practising transcendental meditation who had between six months' and three years' experience. (See Appendix.)

It would be unwise to base too much on this resemblance. No detailed studies of the metabolic rate in Zen meditation have, so far as I know, been published, and there may well be many physiological differences between this practice and transcendental meditation. So far as the electro-encephalographic findings go, however, there does appear to be a similarity; the implication is that transcendental meditation and the Zen practice produce like physiological states, but that transcendental meditation is much more efficient.

This raises the whole question of the uniqueness of transcendental meditation. Is there only one way to reach the state of pure awareness? The answer to this question is both yes and no.

Given the structure of the mind which I have put forward, the only way to reach the state of pure awareness is to go through all the intervening depths of mind, from surface to deepest layers. Transcendental meditation is this diving. Hence there *can* be no other way.

How, then, are we to account for the existence of so many other techniques, all of which claim success?

Such techniques usually fall into one of two broad categories: thinking *about* a subject, which Maharishi compares to swimming on the surface of the pool instead of diving within (and which the Catholic treatises call 'meditation'); and a rather heterogeneous group of practices which includes what the Catholic writers call 'contemplation' and also such techniques as gazing at an object and 'watching the breath'.

People practising any of the techniques in the second group often report some degree of success. This will not be surprising if one remembers that the tendency to experience finer states of thought and to transcend thought is innate; it is the very nature of the mind. *Any* technique is thus likely to lead to transcending; indeed, people may transcend without using any technique at all, and even against their will, as happened to Symonds.

The uniqueness of transcendental meditation thus lies in its effectiveness and in its freedom from extraneous elements. It is meditation's quintessence.

Most other systems stress the need for 'mind control'. The idea is that, because pure awareness is a state without thoughts, the right way to achieve it is to force the mind to become blank. Any success that such methods achieve seems to occur when the mind, tiring of its attempts at concentration, 'lets go' and slips into finer regions of thought. At best, therefore, they represent a roundabout way of achieving what transcendental meditation does directly and naturally.

Of course, the phrase 'mind control' begs the question of who is to do the controlling. It can hardly be the Self, for the fundamental tenet of the Upanishads is that the Self neither acts nor is acted upon; it is a witness only.[1] In reality, the whole idea of control is based upon a misconception. Meditation consists, not in trying to achieve something, but in letting things take their course. Maharishi has put it like this. 'Meditation does not unfold the Self—the Self . . . unfolds Itself, by Itself, to Itself. The mind does nothing to the sun; it only clears away the clouds and the sun is found shining by its own light.' (*BG*, VI, 5.)

The ease with which transcendental meditation is learned and

[1] The same problem in a different form arises for Theravada Buddhism, which, like Hume, denies the existence of a Self altogether.

practised is at once its strength and its weakness. Many people are understandably reluctant to believe that anything which is allegedly so effective could be totally without effort, and they therefore doubt the ease of practice or the efficacy—until they are convinced by experience. It is natural, I suppose, to feel that anything which does not demand effort must be inferior; as a rule only worthless things are obtained without effort. Yet what is one to say? I can only repeat that my own experience, such as it is, as well as that of thousands of other people throughout the world, supports the truth of Maharishi's contention that the way to Self-realization is through *not* trying for it.

Some techniques and some authorities emphasize control much more than others, and indeed a few approach the principle of transcendental meditation. Abbot Chapman provides a good example of a modern Christian writer who has glimpsed part— but only part—of the principle, and I shall discuss his ideas at some length in Chapter XI. Here I should like to point out only that, where transcendental meditation is concerned, a miss is as good as a mile. True, the technique is automatic and effortless; yet, paradoxically, the slightest deviation or misunderstanding and at once everything is lost. The technique must be understood completely or else one is floundering in darkness.

Of the older, Eastern, texts, one of the most interesting is the *Tibetan Book of the Great Liberation*. This remarkable work, which is, significantly, attributed to an Indian teacher who visited Tibet in the eighth century, deals with the state of pure awareness as universal mind. It does not, of course, provide detailed instructions for meditation; these are always given individually. It does, however, contain the striking sentence (my italics): 'This meditation, *devoid of mental concentration*, all-embracing, free from every imperfection, is the most excellent of meditations.' (Op. cit., ed. Evans-Wentz, Oxford, p. 220.)

Jung's commentary on the text is also of the greatest interest, since it reveals both the strength and weakness of this profoundly original thinker. As one would expect, he analyses the text with great sympathy and perceptiveness, but he reaches an impasse at the critical question of oneness of mind. This, he feels, must be the logical end-result of 'lowering the conscious level'. 'But,' he goes on, 'we are unable to imagine how such a realization could ever be complete in any human individual. There must always be somebody or something left over to experience the realization, to say "I know at-one-ment, I know there is no distinction". . . . One cannot know something that is not distinct from oneself. Even when I say "I know myself", as infinitesimal ego—the knowing "I" is still distinct from "myself". In this as it were atomic ego, which is completely ignored by the essentially non-dualist standpoint of the East, there nevertheless lies hidden the whole unabolished pluralistic universe and its unconquered reality. The experience of at-one-ment is . . . an intuition of what it would be like if one could exist and not exist at the same time . . . but for my part I cannot conceive of such a possibility. I therefore assume that, in this point, Eastern intuition has overreached itself.' (Ibid., pp. lx–lxi.)

Jung's thesis is that the 'One Mind' is to be equated with the collective unconscious. This works out reasonably well up to a point, but it fails completely at the level of pure awareness. I think we can accept that Jung's 'collective unconscious' does indeed have some bearing on the scheme of mind which I have adopted. It corresponds, in fact, to the middle regions of the mind-ocean. However, Jung's refusal to accept the reality of the state of pure awareness not only fails to take account of the large number of people who report having reached this state; it also stems from an unjustifiable assumption—that whatever is inconceivable intellectually can have no validity. The text itself makes the best possible comment on this: 'Not knowing the One Mind, even *pundits* go astray, despite their cleverness in expounding the many different doctrinal systems.' (Ibid., p. 237.)

And yet Jung has hit on a most important point when he says that 'the whole unabolished pluralistic universe' lies hidden within the 'atomic ego'. There is here a fundamental paradox: on the one hand the world is multiform; on the other, it is one. Consider the 'intuition of what it would be like if one could exist and not exist at the same time', and compare it with the quotation from Tennyson on p. 49. Individuality, Tennyson says, dissolves and fades away; yet the loss of personality is, not extinction, but the only true life. This, too, is paradoxical. The state of pure awareness, in fact, holds within itself, like a super-saturated solution, the whole universe, ready to crystallize out at a touch.

Over the next few chapters, it is the implications of this fundamental paradox that will be occupying our attention.

# CHAPTER IV

## *Cosmic Consciousness*

WHILE I WAS in Persia I visited a dervish, a Sufi recluse, who lives, or lived, in a converted cave on the outskirts of Shiraz. He was known simply as 'Baba Kuhi' ('Dad of the Mountain'); in fact, he must have been in his thirties, but the title was traditional. The original Baba Kuhi, the author of a fairly well-known book of mystical poems, lived several centuries ago, and his tomb, a black slab covered with inscribed verses, is still to be seen in the cave.

Baba Kuhi made a strong impression on me of peace, of 'sanctity' even, but what I principally remember him for is one remark. Pari or I must have said something expressing wistful envy of his way of life. He gestured towards the city of Shiraz spread out below us like a Persian carpet. 'If everyone lived as I do, how would the world go on?' he asked.

At the time this seemed unanswerable, yet not altogether satisfying, for one part of me hankered after the recluse way of life. Only much later, after I had begun to practise transcendental meditation, did I understand that what matters is inner peace, not outer; and inner peace, to be worth anything, must be proof against all outer circumstances; otherwise it is only a mood.

Transcendental meditation is certainly concerned with inner peace; but this is a conception which can lead to much misunderstanding. Sometimes it is thought to afford an excuse for selfish detachment and withdrawal from life. In reality it is something quite different; the gaining of enlightenment is a process that does not merely tolerate, but demands, activity.

This is a far-reaching and revolutionary principle. Meditation is usually associated in people's minds with tranquillity and withdrawal, and so far as it goes this idea is correct. But it is only a half-truth, and it should not lead one to infer that meditation and activity are somehow incompatible. The view that they are incompatible is deeply ingrained today in both East and West, and has not unnaturally led to a rejection of meditation by most Westerners. We tend to assume that meditation can only be justified—if it can be justified at all—by its effects on everyday living.

Now Maharishi is wholly in agreement with this; indeed, as I have said, he goes further and regards activity as an essential part of the process of gaining enlightenment. This is not for him a question of ethics in the ordinary sense, however, but rather it depends on the structure and function of the nervous system. To explain this I shall have to go a little further into the mechanism of meditation as it relates to activity.

In the last chapter I mentioned that it is the body that calls the diver back to the surface after a dive. It might seem that the return to the surface was something to be regretted. In fact, however, it is not only inevitable; it is the path to further development.

During each meditation, then, there is an alternation between lessening and increasing activity—the two components of every dive. So, too, in life as a whole: meditation, like sleep, affords a regular period of rest in contrast to the activity of daily life. Maharishi sees this alternation between rest and activity as a ubiquitous feature of life; and I think most biologists would agree with him that rhythmicity is a fundamental characteristic of living organisms. Every organ, every tissue, every cell seems to have its phases of activity and rest. For example, a nerve fibre, once stimulated, cannot carry a second impulse until a finite period of time has elapsed; a muscle fibre, likewise, will not respond to the second of two stimuli which reach it too close together. The eyes constantly make fine movements which prevent the image on the retina from remaining in the same place and stimulating the same receptors continuously; if this mechanism is interfered with vision breaks down.

I have already compared meditation to sleep. If the body fails to sleep it will not recover from the strain produced by the day's functioning, and if sleep deprivation continues too long severe mental and physical disorder will result. Maharishi holds that the deep rest which transcendental meditation supplies is a similar biological necessity. 'Stress residues' which lie too deep to be accessible to the healing influence of sleep are removed during the daily periods of meditation.

One way of looking at transcendental meditation, then, is as a technique for allowing the body to take exceptionally deep rest and so to cope better with the problems of living in an increasingly stressful environment. The physiological studies summarized in the Appendix suggest that this is indeed the effect of the meditation.

The enhanced mental capacity and creativity and the release from anxiety which meditators report are presumably the psychological counterparts of this release of physical tension. What one *experiences* is that the mind is no longer caught up in futile thoughts—in neuroses, in fact—but is free to attend to what matters. There are obvious similarities between transcendental meditation, looked at in this way, and psycho-analysis. However, there are also important differences. The principal one is, I think, the respective levels at which meditation and psycho-analysis act. I feel it may be worth making a short digression to bring this out clearly.

Psycho-analysis is a vast and luxuriant jungle, in which any unwary trespasser is almost certain to be lost without trace. I think, however, that I can hazard the general comment that a fundamental postulate of all the various schools is that mental disorder has psychological causes and can be treated psychologically. The question remains whether all psychological disorders have some physical basis. In other words, are there anatomical or chemical changes in the brains of people suffering from, say, claustrophobia or obsessional neurosis? Freud himself certainly believed that there were, although Jung was more doubtful. For almost all modern neurophysiologists there is no doubt at all; for them it is more or less an article of faith that every mental event *must* have a physical counterpart. (And Maharishi, as I have said, agrees with this.)

In recent years the trend in the treatment of mental disorders has been towards physical and chemical methods. In Great Britain especially, but also in the United States, psycho-analysis has been under attack on both theoretical and practical grounds. Critics such as H. J. Eysenck have contended that even if neuroses are caused in the ways that Freud claimed, this is irrelevant to their treatment. Thus, instead of looking for the original cause of a patient's symptoms, psychiatrists of this persuasion attempt to treat the symptom itself. This trend is in line with the swing towards more physical methods which is evident in the immense increase in the prescribing of 'tranquillizers' and anti-depressants, especially by hard-pressed general practitioners, that has been such a feature of the last few years.

Where does transcendental meditation stand in relation to all this? Undoubtedly it is closer to the 'physical' pole. Suppose we accept that all psychological dysfunction has a physical basis in the nervous system, however difficult this may be to prove. (If you do not accept it you are not necessarily wrong, but you are outside the pale so far as modern scientific orthodoxy is concerned.) The original cause of this physical abnormality may have been anything—any sufficiently strong stimulus, including the 'traumas' of the psycho-analysts. What happens during meditation, according to Maharishi, is that the body goes into a state of deep *physical* rest, and in this state the *physical* abnormalities are removed. (Admittedly this is still to a large extent a hypothesis, though it is in no worse case in this respect than most other claims made about psychology. However, there is already a little 'hard' evidence to support the hypothesis; see the findings concerning blood lactate levels described in the Appendix.) The result of this on the *psychological* level is a release from the burden of neurosis—anxiety, obsession, and so forth.

There is no necessary challenge here to the elaborate theories of symbolism developed by Freud and Jung; these will continue to stand or fall on their own merits. I myself believe that Jung, in particular, saw deeply into the mechanism of the 'unconscious'. But meditation is a short cut; it by-passes all the delving into the unconscious upon which Jung's system of psychotherapy depends.

Still more important, transcendental meditation goes to a much deeper level than does psycho-analysis. It goes, in fact, to the level of pure awareness, which Jung expressly declared to be non-existent (see p. 63). That is, it brings man into contact with his own Being.

The psychological theory which is of undoubted relevance here is that of Abraham Maslow, who actually talks of a psychology of Being (See *Toward a Psychology of Being*, 2nd ed., Van Nostrand Reinhold.) Among the fundamental postulates of Maslow's psychology are the following. Each of us has an essential inner nature, which is 'instinctoid', intrinsic, given. This inner nature is *not* necessarily evil; it is either neutral or positively good (Maslow is not sure which). Destructiveness, sadism, cruelty, and so on seem not to be intrinsic but rather to be reactions *against* frustrations of our inner needs, emotions, and capacities. The way to live a healthy, fruitful, happy life is not to frustrate our inner nature but to bring it out and encourage it. If we do try to suppress it, the result will be sickness—sometimes obvious, sometimes subtle.

These assumptions, Maslow believes, offer 'a scientific ethics, a natural value system, a court of ultimate appeal for the determination of good and bad, of right and wrong. The more we learn about man's natural tendencies, the easier it will be to tell him how to be good, how to be happy, how to be fruitful, how to respect himself, how to love, how to fulfil his highest potentialities. This amounts to automatic solution of many of the personality problems of the future. The thing to do seems to be to find out what one is *really* like inside, deep down, as a member of the human species and as a particular individual.' (Op. cit., p. 85.)

This last sentence in particular reads almost like a prescription for transcendental meditation. And the results of 'finding out' are also extraordinarily like the results of practising transcendental meditation. They are what Maslow calls self-actualization. 'Self-actualization is defined in various ways but a solid core of agreement is perceptible. All definitions accept or imply (a) acceptance and expression of the inner core or self, i.e. actualization of these latent capacities and potentialities, "full functioning", availability of the human and personal essence. (b) They all imply minimal presence of ill health, neurosis, psychosis, of loss or diminution of the basic human and personal capacities.' (Ibid., p. 197.) Other important components of self-actualization are a certain lightness or 'playfulness' and creativity (on which see Chapter X.)

Self-actualization, we are told, is a rare achievement; only about one per cent of the population attains it. The principal means of fostering it is psychotherapy. Here, of course, there is a point of difference from transcendental meditation. However, there is a point of close connection in Maslow's interest in 'peak experiences'. These are, at their highest state of development, brief flashes of the higher states of consciousness described by Maharishi (see Chapter VII). Peak experiences are enjoyed with unusual frequency and completeness by self-actualizing people; they also help self-actualization to occur.

Maslow's discussion of peak experiences, and indeed the whole of his book, is of the greatest interest from the point of view of transcendental meditation. Perhaps I could summarize this by saying that transcendental meditation is a direct path to self-actualization *and beyond*. For self-knowledge can be even more complete and far-reaching than Maslow implies. *Full* self-actualization means bringing out and using not only the inner nature of which Maslow speaks but also the inmost nature of all—the inner pure awareness.

Notice that as we come closer and closer to this inmost Self, it becomes harder and harder to find words to describe it. We are driven increasingly towards metaphor. This is not because the Self is unreal—on the contrary, it is the supreme reality—but because it is at the limit of 'subtlety'. At this level words lose their grip. As the Upanishads say, it is difficult to describe the Self except by negations.

Hence the need for metaphors. One can say that as the psychophysical tensions that cloud awareness are progressively released through meditation, the Self begins to shine through more brightly. Another way of putting it would be to say that the nervous system, the reflector of consciousness, is being polished until it can reflect the omnipresent pure awareness.

Yet another metaphor which Maharishi often uses in this context is 'infusion of Being'. Being, or pure awareness, soaks in from the deepest layers of the mind, like ink into a strip of blotting paper; and it reaches the superficial levels of awareness last of all. That is why, although changes occur right from the start, the meditator himself often does not notice them—although his friends and relatives usually do. One cannot generalize, but often the changes are more apparent to others than to oneself. Certainly, to keep watching anxiously for changes is a mistake, since the personality grows and evolves as a whole. A child does not notice his own growth from day to day. Transcendental meditation is like this; not a matter of sudden leaps but a natural organic process.

The process of infusion depends, as I have said, on alternation between the silence of meditation and the movement of activity; both sides of our nature, Mary and Martha, have to be fulfilled. Maharishi illustrates this point with an analogy. When cloth was to be dyed with the old vegetable dyes the cloth was dipped in the dye and was brought out fully coloured, but the dye was not fast. To make it so the dyers exposed it to the sun and allowed it to fade; then it was dyed and exposed once more. The process was continued until the dye no longer faded when exposed to the sun. Both the dipping and the fading were needed to make the dye fast. Similarly, if the effects of meditation are to be stabilized they must, paradoxically, be allowed to be dissipated in activity.

The importance of activity in relation to transcendental meditation cannot be over-emphasized. As one comes out of meditation the mind is still infused with something of the silence of pure awareness. As the day wears on this silence fades; yet not wholly. And at the next meditation it is renewed. As I said at the beginning of this chapter, the only inner peace which is worth anything is that which persists in all circumstances. Maharishi therefore insists that meditators should act in the world without trying to maintain the silence of meditation, for it is precisely by passing from one state to the other—from silence to activity and back again—that one becomes accustomed to both; and more than that, one begins to maintain the state of pure awareness along with activity.

Here is yet another fresh insight on Maharishi's part. Many systems and teachers enjoin 'continual mindfulness'—that is, the attempt to preserve the effects of meditation outside the time of meditation. In Maharishi's understanding this has no place. Outside meditation one leads a normal life, just as one did before, and *one does not need to think about meditation at all*. And this is because the aim of transcendental meditation is to modify, not merely thinking itself, but the mechanism which supports thinking—the nervous system.

To explain what this means I shall have to go back to an idea which I introduced in Chapter II. There I illustrated the nature of pure awareness with the analogy of a cinema screen, and I tried to show that we ordinarily take our sense of identity, not from the underlying reality of the screen, but from the shifting pattern of images that plays upon it. This idea could be taken further and represented in almost cybernetic terms. Our sense of identity depends on the integrity of a cycle of perception, recognition-desire, and action. An impression reaches the mind (the brain, if you prefer) via the senses; there it 'resonates' with stored impressions (memories) and the combination of impression and memory reaches awareness as a desire. The desire, in turn, may manifest itself as an action; and satisfaction of the desire will reinforce the cycle, so acting as the seed of future desire. This is obviously a summary account of a complex process, but the essential point I wish to make is that the empirical ego depends upon this cycle for its very existence. Disturb the functioning of one or more of the elements in the cycle and you have mental illness. Interrupt the cycle artificially —by experimental sensory deprivation, for instance—and there result hallucinations; frequently there is a loss of the feeling of personal identity. (Brain-washing techniques are largely based on this principle.) Our ordinary sense of identity depends on the integrity of the cycle. The fear of death is at root a fear that the cycle will be broken.

During transcendental meditation the cycle is allowed to run down temporarily, and in this way the experiencer is left alone with nothing to experience; this is transcendental consciousness, pure awareness. The return to the ordinary waking state means that the cycle starts to revolve once more, and pure awareness is again obscured. With continual repetition of the swing from activity to rest and back again, however, a time eventually comes when both transcendental awareness and activity in the relative phase can exist simultaneously.

*To this state of dual awareness Maharishi gives the name 'cosmic consciousness'. Once fully gained it is permanent and is maintained spontaneously throughout the waking, dreaming, and sleeping phases.*

This is certainly a difficult concept to put into words. Throughout this chapter I have had constant recourse to metaphor and analogy, and this is inevitable, for the 'subtler' states of awareness are by definition pre-verbal, while the state of pure awareness is 'pre-everything'. If this is difficult to imagine, the state in which pure awareness and relative ordinary awareness are lived simultaneously is even more inconceivable! As Maharishi has said: 'When the eternal silence of the unmanifest is joined in living experience with the eternal activity of the manifest, not at distinct times but concurrently, then is experienced that which is beyond words. If we try to render the state into words we find ourselves descending into absurdity.' (*Meditation*, SRM Publications, p. 37.)

Cosmic consciousness, then, is a paradox, but one that is lived, as the Bhagavad Gita insists, 'with ease'. And this is because it depends upon a physiological modification of the nervous system. Coming to the state of pure awareness is, as we have seen, accompanied by quite distinctive physiological changes. Just as the waking, dreaming, and deep sleep states depend for their existence upon certain definite dispositions of the nervous system, so too there must be a disposition of the nervous system corresponding to the state of pure awareness. This disposition Maharishi refers to as 'restful alertness'. Cosmic consciousness will depend on the maintenance of the condition of restful alertness together with the condition responsible for the waking, dreaming, or deep sleep state, as the case may be.

It is not, of course, possible to say what are the precise modifications undergone by the nervous system in cosmic consciousness. One suggestion is that some area of the nervous system which is at present unused or under-used may come into play; the frontal lobes might be candidates here, for the function of these large 'silent' areas of the brain is still almost unknown. Another possibility is suggested by some recent findings in porpoises. According to Professor V. B. Mountcastle (*BCE*, p. 382), porpoises close one eye at a time and sleep with each cerebral hemisphere alternately; in this way they can remain swimming at all times. Here we have the nervous system of a mammal (and porpoises have highly evolved brains, larger and more convoluted than those of man) maintaining two states simultaneously. Could something analogous occur in cosmically conscious man?

On the other hand, it may well be that all such ideas are too crude, and we should be thinking in terms of increase in the complexity of the hierarchical structure of the nervous system. Sperry's thinking leads in this direction in the following interesting passage.

'The "search for psyche" in my own case at least has been directed mainly at higher-level configurations of the brain like specialized circuit systems—and not just any juicy central nerve network that happens to be complex and teeming with electrical excitation. I have been inclined to look rather at circuits specifically designed for the express job of producing effects like pain, or high C, or blue-yellow, circuits of the kind that one finds above a high transection of the spinal cord, but not below—circuits with something that may well be present in the tiny pinhead dimensions of the midbrain of the colour-perceiving goldfish, but lacking in the massive spinal-cord tissue of the ox, circuits that are profoundly affected by certain lesions of the midbrain and thalamus, but remarkably little altered by complete absence of the entire human cerebellum. And if it actually came to laying money on the line, I would probably bet first choice on still larger cerebral configurations, configurations that include the combined effects of both (a) the specialized circuit systems like the foregoing, plus (b) a background of cerebral activity of the alert waking type. Take away the specific circuit, or the background, or the orderly activity from either one, and the conscious effect is gone.' (*BCE*, p. 307.)

And if one added a new, even larger, 'cerebral configuration', would one perhaps get cosmic consciousness? Maharishi himself seems to feel that something like this is a possibility, as he brings out in this passage from his commentary on the Bhagavad Gita (IV, 38):

'This gradual and systematic culture of the physical nervous system creates a physiological situation in which the two states [sc. waking and transcendental] of consciousness exist together simultaneously. It is well known that there exist in the nervous system many autonomous levels of function, between which a system of coordination also exists. In the state of cosmic consciousness two different levels of organization in the nervous system function simultaneously while maintaining their separate identities. By virtue of this anatomical separation of function, it becomes possible for transcendental consciousness to co-exist with the waking state of consciousness and with the dreaming and sleeping states of consciousness.

'In the early stages of the practice of transcendental meditation, these two levels of function in the nervous system are unable to occur at the same time; the function of the one inhibits the function of the other. That is why, at this stage, either transcendental consciousness or the waking state of consciousness is experienced. The practice of the mind in passing from one to another gradually overcomes this physiological inhibition, and the two levels begin to function perfectly at the same time, without inhibiting each other and still maintaining their separate identities. The function of each is independent of the other, and that is why this state of the nervous system corresponds to cosmic consciousness, in which Self-awareness exists as separate from activity. Silence is experienced with activity and yet as separate from it.'

I find this an interesting suggestion, because we do in fact know that there are two anatomically and functionally separate parts of the nervous system, each responsible for different aspects of consciousness. 'Neurology lends support to the distinction between the content of consciousness and the state of consciousness itself. The content of consciousness consists of sensations, emotions, images, memories, ideas, and similar experiences, and these depend upon the activities of the cerebral cortex and the thalamus and the relations between them, in the sense that lesions of these structures alter the content of consciousness without as a rule changing the state of consciousness as such. On the other hand, recent work has shown that other structures, particularly that part of the central reticular formation of the brain stem, which is known as the ascending reticular activating system ... profoundly influence the state of consciousness.' (Brain's *Diseases of the Nervous System* [7th Edition], revised by the late Lord Brain and John N. Walton, pp. 965–6.) The cortex receives at least two kinds of impulse; some activate specific areas (those concerned with sight, hearing, and so on, while others alter the activity of the cortex as a whole. One can destroy the reticulo-hypothalamic system while leaving the sensory impulses free to arrive at the cortex. In this case there are no conscious processes, because the tonic impulses from the reticulo-hypothalamic system are absent. Drugs such as anaesthetics and hypnotics appear to produce unconsciousness by reducing the activity of the ascending reticular alerting system, while stimulants have the opposite effect.

It is an attractive hypothesis to suppose that during meditation the activity of the thalamo-cortical system (responsible for the content of consciousness) is reduced, while that of the reticulo-thalamic system (responsible for alertness) is maintained. One might further speculate that cosmic consciousness consists in a permanent modification in the amount or character of the activity of the reticulo-thalamic system.

But of course all these speculations are no more than that—speculations. After all, we know almost nothing of the way ordinary consciousness, let alone cosmic consciousness, is maintained. But whatever the actual mechanism may be, there is, I think, no inherent difficulty in supposing that modification of the nervous system can occur. Indeed, modern theories of memory (inadequate though all of them are) all postulate some change in cerebral structure, chemistry, or electrical state as the basis of the memory trace. Again, there is evidence that exposure to a 'stimulus-rich' environment changes the brains of rats by increasing both the content of ribonucleic acid and the complexity of interneuronal connections. Finally, experience of drugs such as LSD shows that tiny amounts of certain substances can produce far-reaching changes in the way the brain works.

In conclusion, one point needs stressing. Maharishi insists that cosmic consciousness is not anything strange or abnormal, but is simply *Self*-awareness; and the condition of the nervous system which allows it to exist is the 'normal' condition. What is abnormal is the *absence* of cosmic consciousness. To put this in the terms which I used earlier: transcendental meditation is a means of removing the physical basis of psychological dysfunction, and when this has been done the state of clear awareness called cosmic consciousness necessarily results. In Maslow's terminology, cosmic consciousness is full self-actualization; it represents a coming to fruition of all the latent powers of the individual.

Thus, for anyone to say 'transcendental meditation is fine for some people, but I don't need it' is absurd; for what benefit can there be in not making use of all the possibilities open to one?

# CHAPTER V

## *Ethics and Free Will*

COSMIC CONSCIOUSNESS IS a key concept in Maharishi's philosophy. Indeed, so far as I know it is unique to Maharishi; no one before him, I think, has described this state clearly.[1] Its importance is that it is a clue to unravel the otherwise remarkably confusing question of 'higher states of consciousness'. This will be my concern over the next few chapters; but first I should like to go a little further into some of the implications of cosmic consciousness for our understanding of ourselves and the world. To do this, I shall have to say something about Maharishi's philosophy of action, but here a warning is necessary. I have not attempted to present a full or even an adequate summary of his views on this most important topic, because it seems to me that this could only be done by someone who was himself in large measure 'enlightened'. Maharishi's own exposition of this central part of his teaching will be found in his commentary on Chapters IV and V of the Bhagavad Gita, and these are essential reading for anyone who hopes to get a clear grasp of his ideas.

However, the kernel of the matter can be simply stated. The Bhagavad Gita puts it as follows:

'One who is in Union with the Divine and who knows the truth will maintain "I do not act at all". In seeing, hearing, touching, smelling, eating, walking, sleeping, breathing, letting go, seizing, and even in opening and closing the eyes, he holds simply that the senses act among the objects of sense.' (V, 8–9.)

Here is Maharishi's gloss on this:

'The authorship of action does not in reality belong to the "I". It is a mistake to understand that "I" do this, "I" experience this and "I" know this. All this is basically untrue. The "I", in its essential nature, is uncreated; it belongs to the field of the Absolute. Whereas action, its fruits and the relationship between

[1] R. M. Bucke uses the term cosmic consciousness in his book of that name, but in quite a different way.

the doer and his action belong to the relative field, to the field of the three gunas [sc. the forces of nature]. Therefore all action is performed by the three gunas born of Nature. The attribution of authorship to the "I" is only due to ignorance of the real nature of the "I" and of action.' (*BG*, V, 14, commentary.)

The implications of these passages are tremendous—and admittedly hard to take in on the first encounter. What Maharishi is saying is that in cosmic consciousness the nature of the Self is appreciated as it is—that is, separate from activity. On the one hand 'I' am unchanging, eternal, uninvolved with activity; on the other, activity continues.

Here we have the constantly reiterated theme of the Bhagavad Gita. 'Liberation', the goal of so many systems, past and present, does not consist in achieving anything or reaching anything, but simply in recognizing what already is the case; that the true 'I' is essentially uninvolved with activity.

This is a purely subjective affair. The cosmically conscious man does not, Maharishi insists, behave any differently from anyone else. He still has his likes and dislikes; above all, he continues to act. True, he is likely to appear a well-integrated person, but that is all. The only criterion is internal: is the Self cognized as independent of activity?

Maharishi compares the experiences of an unenlightened man to a line engraved in stone. As one continues to meditate experiences become like a line drawn on sand: and in cosmic consciousness they are like a line drawn on water. The enlightened man is not without emotions, but these are perceived as not touching the Self. This is because the bliss of Self-awareness is so firmly infused into the mind that it overshadows pleasure and sorrow alike.

It is important to understand that in all this there is no loss. Nothing is taken away; on the contrary, there is an immense gain—the gain of awareness of the Self. This is what Tennyson described (p. 49) as the 'only true life'. The gaining of cosmic consciousness is 'liberation', because in this state the true self is found to be free from the limitations of the relative world. The state which exists before liberation—the state in which we ordinarily live—is called 'bondage' or 'identification' because in it the self is *not* clearly separated from the relative world, and hence one wrongly identifies one's self with the physical body and with one's emotions and desires.

This concept of liberation may seem to raise difficulties from the standpoint of ethics. If I am not the author of my actions, does it not follow that I am not responsible for them and may do whatever I please? Is not Maharishi preaching irresponsible hedonism or even antinomianism? The picture which emerges is of the cosmically conscious as enjoying a permanent Bacchanal —enlivened, presumably, by *tableaux vivants* inspired by the Kama Sutra.

Antinomian tendencies have appeared at times in many religions, perhaps in most. They seem to follow periods of great enlightenment; and they are, I think, yet another example of misinterpreting teachings that can only be understood at a certain level of enlightenment. Now, a cardinal feature of Maharishi's view of the path of development is that everyone must act from his own level of consciousness. Hence the descriptions of how a cosmically conscious man acts should not be taken for precepts. The invariable rule is that the quality of one's actions depend on the level of one's awareness and never the reverse.

Maharishi maintains that truly ethical action is only possible in the state of enlightenment, because in this state—and only in this state—actions are fully and automatically in harmony with the needs of the cosmos; and this for him is the criterion of rightness. The 'ignorant' (which includes most of us!) should follow the norms of their society and, if they have one, their religion. Naturally, however, enlightenment is not an all-or-nothing affair, and as one continues to evolve one's actions become more and more ethical.[1]

The corollary of all this is that no amount of virtuous action will, by itself, produce cosmic consciousness. Enlightenment results from a particular condition of the nervous system, which

---

[1] The philosophy of ethics is almost as contentious as the free-will problem. For my part, I agree with those who hold that ethical questions can never be finally decided by reason alone. Our knowledge of right and wrong is ultimately intuitive. (True, most of it is handed down to us from earlier generations, but tradition itself is in the end based on past intuitions.) The question remains, what are we intuiting? The answer, I think, is something like cosmic law. To act more morally we need, not keener intellects, but subtler intuition.

is produced by the regular alternation of deep rest and activity; it is not the consequence of right action. Maharishi believes firmly that generations of moralists, in the East as well as in the West, have in this respect been putting the cart before the horse.

Another question which, it seems to me, is raised in an acute form by Maharishi's teaching is the notion of individual freedom. For clearly the concept of cosmic consciousness has a great deal of relevance to the problem of free will.

The free-will controversy is, as John Beloff has remarked, one of the most notorious quicksands in the whole of philosophy, and I am certainly not going to be so rash as to try to discuss it in detail. However, Beloff provides a convenient summary of the principal arguments (see *The Existence of Mind*, MacGibbon & Kee, 1962, pp. 140–74), and I think he correctly indentifies the crux of the whole problem when he says that the basic difficulty is to understand the very meaning of free will.

The dilemma arises in the following way. A choice is either determined or it is not. If it is determined, it is not free. But if it is not determined, to what are we to ascribe it? To chance?

Some people have indeed tried to relate free will to quantum theory. If the events at the sub-atomic levels in our brains are not determined in the classic sense—which is what Heisenberg's famous principle of indeterminacy implies—then perhaps it is these sub-atomic events which govern our actions. In this way our actions would be, as it were, salted by chance; and it would be this unpredictability which we appreciate as free will.

This theory has grave flaws. For one thing, we do not know whether sub-atomic events in the brain do really influence the comparatively gross neural events that cause our actions. For another, the indeterminacy principle itself may eventually turn out to be mistaken; among physicists who have believed this have been de Broglie, Schrödinger, and Einstein.

But in any case, would a 'freedom' that depended on nothing more than chance be any better than a thorough-going determinism? To say that our actions have *no* cause would surely be as unacceptable as to say that they are wholly determined.

An interesting approach to the problem has been made by

Sperry. He cannot, he says, find any alternative to causal determinism; but he feels that perhaps this may not be such a disaster after all. The solution he advocates is acceptance. 'If you can't lick 'em, join 'em. If we cannot avoid determinism, accept and work with it. There may be worse "fates" than causal determinism. Maybe after all it is better to be properly embedded in the causal flow of cosmic forces, as an integral part thereof, than to be on the loose and to have no antecedent cause and hence no reason or any reliability for future plans or predictions. . . . If one were assigned the task of trying to design and build the perfect free-will model . . . consider the possibility that instead of trying to *free* the machinery from causal contact, it might be better perhaps to aim at the opposite: that is, to try to incorporate into the model the value of *universal contact*; in other words, contact with all related information in proper proportion—past, present, and future.' (*BCE*, p. 305.) The trend of evolution, Sperry goes on to suggest, is indeed in the direction of such 'universal causal contact'.

So far as it goes, this is fine. We are part of the universe, and therefore, whether we like it or not and whether we are aware of it or not, all our actions are determined by the total effect of cosmic forces. This is precisely what Maharishi means when he says 'all action is performed by the three gunas born of Nature'. But this account leaves something unexplained: our inner sense of freedom. Why should we have this obstinate sense that somehow, in spite of everything, we are not helpless in the grip of impersonal fate?

As so often happens, it is Schrödinger who comes up with an illuminating idea. Science, he agrees, leads quite uncompromisingly to the view that the body is a pure mechanism, functioning in accordance with the laws of nature. So far the determinists are correct; there is no need to postulate a 'vital force'. Nevertheless, my conviction of inner freedom is equally certain; I know incontrovertibly, from my own inner experience, that I direct the motions of my body; I foresee the effects of my actions, and feel and take full responsibility for them. In other words, *both* determinism *and* free will seem to be true. Here we have two apparently contradictory statements, both true. How can they be reconciled?

Schrödinger's answer is breathtakingly bold. 'The only possible inference from these two facts is, I think, that I—I in the widest meaning of the word, that is to say, every conscious mind that has ever said or felt "I"—am the person, if any, who controls the "motion of the atoms" according to the Laws of Nature.' (*What is Life?*, pp. 92–3.)

What we have arrived at here—as Schrödinger himself points out—is the great insight of the Upanishads: Atman (the individual Self) is the same as Brahman (the Self of the universe).

This tremendous claim goes beyond what is found to be the case even in cosmic consciousness, and this is a point I shall return to in more detail later. But even at this stage certain conclusions emerge so far as the free-will question is concerned.

In the first place, it appears that the paradox must remain a paradox on the level of 'ignorance'. At this level both determinism and free will are true, and the difference between them is largely a matter of standpoint—subjectively I feel free, but intellectual analysis tells me I am not.

But secondly, even on the level of cosmic consciousness the problem is not 'solved', although it is seen in a different light. In cosmic consciousness one perceives that action depends on impersonal forces (the laws of nature) but one also perceives that one's Self is not involved with this play of forces; hence one is free. Thus it could be said that in the state of ignorance the free-will paradox is in solution, detectable only by intellectual analysis, whereas in cosmic consciousness it has visibly crystallized out and cannot be missed. As one might expect, the dawning of cosmic consciousness could well be a puzzling experience for someone who did not understand what was going on, and so a teacher is necessary. As we saw in the case of Symonds, even the state of pure awareness can be frightening if one does not understand it.

It seems to me that the concept of cosmic consciousness, when applied to the free-will problem, affords a remarkable degree of clarification of an ancient puzzle. But admittedly it does so at what may well seem to some people a high price—the introduction of the 'mystical' notion of a universal self.

At this point I have, as it were, to change gear. Up to now I have been treating pure awareness and cosmic consciousness as if they were entirely subjective, with no relevance to the outer world. From now on, however, I have to put them in a wider context, and try to show how these altered states of awareness serve as keys to an understanding of the world as a whole.

This can be an extraordinarily difficult step for a Westerner to take. We are so conditioned to making a rigid distinction between subjective and objective that the idea of there possibly being common ground on which they meet is almost inconceivable to us. On the one hand, we feel, there is the outer world of objects, and on the other the inner world of feelings and ideas, and the two have little to say to each other. Moreover, since the triumph of the scientific method we have the feeling that to label something as subjective is to devalue it; only the objective world is quite respectable. And surely the state of pure awareness is 'merely' subjective, and hence of no use as a basis for a knowledge of reality?

For the main stream of Indian philosophy, however, as well as for a minority of Western philosophers (probably including Plato), to reach the state of pure awareness is to come into contact with the Absolute, the source of all that is. Now, this may seem a wildly metaphysical notion, incompatible with a scientific world view. So it is important to make clear that the concept of an Absolute is not intended as a *deus ex machina*; no supernatural agency is being invoked. The world remains subject to natural law. There is no violation of what Stace has called the naturalistic principle, which implies that all macroscopic existences and events occurring in the space-time world are explicable without exception by natural causes. (Maharishi has said that miracles are natural events whose causes we do not understand.)

The concept of the Absolute is in no sense inconsistent with the naturalistic principle. Indeed, one might go further. One aim of scientific enquiry is to provide more comprehensive, and at the same time simpler and more elegant, explanations of natural phenomena. The Absolute represents the end-result of this process. It could, I think, be argued that the whole idea of scientific discovery springs from an intuitive knowledge of the presence of an Absolute.

However, such knowledge can be more than intuitive, and the Absolute need not remain at the level of a hypothesis. But this is such an important topic that it had better have a chapter to itself.

# CHAPTER VI

## *The Absolute*

THE FIRST THING to say about the Absolute is that nothing can be said about it! As the Upanishads put it, Brahman is described by negatives—not this, not that. All positive statements by implication exclude what is not stated, and therefore can never be true of the Absolute, which is all-embracing. However—and this is the crucial paradox—the Absolute does after all have attributes; that is, it manifests itself in certain ways and these manifestations can be looked on as attributes. I shall return to this paradox later. At present I should like to consider each of the so-called attributes of the Absolute in turn.

In Indian philosophy there are said to be three of them: Being (*sat*), consciousness (*chit*), and bliss (*ananda*).

Bliss we have already considered (see p. 52), and there is not much to add at this point. The Absolute is discovered by experience to be blissful, and this is because it represents the dissolution of all tensions and oppositions. One point is perhaps worth making: according to Maharishi, bliss is only experienced at the moment of *contact* with the Absolute. Once one has, as it were, entered the Absolute all differentiation has ceased and so there is no one left to experience bliss. The analogy which comes to my mind is that of a fish which has been taken out of the water and then returned; it might, I suppose, experience joy at the moment it re-entered the water, but once it was swimming in its own element it would cease to feel the contrast.

As we have seen, it is the bliss-attribute of the Absolute which is of such practical importance in transcendental meditation.

Now consciousness. Here we reach what I myself have found a most illuminating idea. For Maharishi, individual consciousness is produced *by the reflection of the Absolute in a given nervous system*. The Absolute itself is, as it were, a mass of pure undifferentiated consciousness, 'waiting' for a nervous system to be able to manifest itself. Here the analogy which occurs to me is that of radio

86

waves, which fill empty space with potential sound that cannot be heard unless there is a suitable receiver. Moreover, the quality of the receiver will affect the sound which reaches one's ears. In the same way, the nervous system does not produce consciousness, but it allows it to become manifest, and the nature of individual awareness depends on the quality of the nervous system which is acting as a reflector.

This may seem to be a total reversal of the currently fashionable view that consciousness is an emergent property of nervous systems and hence indissolubly linked to them. Yet I believe that this picture and Maharishi's can be reconciled; they are largely different ways of looking at the facts. All the known phenomena of neurology can be accommodated perfectly well on the reflector theory. The normal waking, dreaming, and deep sleep phases, for example, will depend on changes in the state of the reflector; similarly, damage to the reflector will inevitably produce distorted reflections of consciousness. The growth of the intellect to maturity, the gradual deterioration of senescence, the more dramatic losses of function caused by disease—all these are explicable. There is thus no difficulty in seeing how it happens that the brain appears to be so fundamental to consciousness. Any change in the state of the brain must inevitably be reflected in the quality of individual consciousness, just as a faulty valve will impair the quality of sound the radio produces.

Yet although the 'reflector' theory can accommodate the findings of physiology perfectly well, it must be admitted that epiphenomenalism would do so equally effectively and more economically. One hears William of Occam sharpening his razor once more. What does the reflector theory offer that epiphenomenalism does not?

In the first place, the reflector theory puts consciousness where most people instinctively feel it belongs—as the primary fact of existence as we know it. No longer relegated to the role of an 'epiphenomenon', consciousness takes its rightful place as the one essential 'given'.[1]

Again, the question whether consciousness exists in animals

---

[1] Yet notice that, on the reflector theory, consciousness is not actually *doing* anything. The Self, according to the Upanishads, neither acts nor is acted upon. Epiphenomenalism thus does contain a grain of truth after all!

is no longer a problem on the reflector theory; and if necessary one could go further. A number of modern philosophers have speculated on the possibility that consciousness, however rudimentary, may not be confined even to living organisms. Sperry, for example, has been led by his research on brain bisection to 'wonder if we can really rule out ... the ... contention of those who maintain that spinal cords, loaves of bread, and even single molecules have a kind of consciousness'. (*BCE*, p. 303.)

Many thinkers throughout the ages have toyed with this kind of panpsychism, but most, especially in modern times, have rejected it, even if reluctantly. One can understand why. It is true that panpsychism seems more in keeping with our general experience of nature, which suggests that new properties do not emerge suddenly as a rule but shade away imperceptibly into those from which they originated and those into which they are developing. It is also true, however, that it is hard for us to think of an inanimate object as in any sense conscious; and many people, including Descartes, have denied consciousness even to animals. To my mind at least, the contradiction between these two views disappears when I think of individual consciousness as a reflection of omnipresent pure awareness. This does not imply that we must credit tables and chairs, atoms and solar systems, with souls; it does however help to bridge the otherwise impassable gap which seems to separate ourselves, as conscious thinking beings, from the rest of nature.

Many ancient controversies lose much of their importance if one thinks of them in this way. There is no point, for example, in asking how far down the evolutionary tree consciousness goes; even the amoeba, presumably, reflects its tiny spark of awareness. So, too, with the development of the individual. How early does the foetus become conscious? *Some* degree of consciousness must be reflected even by the fertilized ovum, and as growth of the brain proceeds reflection becomes clearer and clearer—until, ideally, cosmic consciousness is achieved. But there is no one point at which consciousness can be said suddenly to appear.

Nor is consciousness confined in duration to that split-second of geological time which has witnessed the development of life on this planet. Before the first conglomeration of amino acids that merited the name of a living organism appeared in the 'primeval soup', was the world, in Schrödinger's words, 'a performance to empty stalls'? I agree with Schrödinger that this idea does not make sense. On the reflector theory of consciousness, of course, the anomaly disappears.

The reflector theory of consciousness should be thought of in conjunction with the tripartite scheme of personality which I put forward in Chapter III. On that scheme, you will remember, the 'mind' region is part of the relative world but is intermediate between the physical level (brain) and the Absolute pure awareness. One may conceive of the mind as Janus-like; it faces in two directions, subtler and grosser, simultaneously. From the grosser, physical, aspect it derives, via the senses and brain, its knowledge of the external world,[1] while from the subtler aspect will come thoughts, concepts, and values; and these ultimately all derive from the Absolute, as was held by Plato and many people since. The late Professor Sir Cyril Burt, for example, wrote '. . . I am convinced that there is only *one* basic Order—which appears as logical or mathematical to our cognitive intuition, aesthetic to our emotional intuition, and moral to the

---

[1] If, as I suggested earlier, we conceive of the mind by analogy with field theory, I think we should probably follow a number of psychical researchers, including Sir Cyril Burt, in holding that all perception is a form of clairvoyance. The brain and sense organs would then be filters, screening off unwanted clairvoyant impressions. The Indian view that the physical senses are the grosser aspect of subtler channels of awareness seems to fit in with this idea. Indeed, one finds in the Upanishads the description of an elaborate structure of the personality, from the gross physical level of the body through the mind to the Self (Atman). The 'mind' region is subdivided into senses, mind (*manas*), intellect, and ego. Roughly, these subdivisions function as follows: (1) The senses are related to, but not identical with, the appropriate organs of perception; they are subtler versions of these. (2) The mind, *manas*, is the part connected with thought. (3) Intellect is the faculty of choosing; it is responsible for the direction of flow of thought in *manas*. (4) Ego, which is *not* identical with the ego of Western psychologists, is the 'I' quality of the individual, which simply witnesses the activity of the other elements. In the Upanishadic analogy, the ego is the master of a chariot (*manas*) in which it is a passenger and is being driven by a charioteer (intellect). The horses drawing the chariot are the senses. Thus the intellect controls the direction of the mind, while the ego looks on approvingly or otherwise.

Maharishi explains that this account of the structure of the personality is intended as an aid to understanding and not as a literal description of what goes on. This qualification naturally applies to all models; they are helpful provided they are not pushed too far. In this book I have avoided the temptation to put forward a detailed structure of the 'mind' region, but an interesting attempt to do so by P. J. Russell can be found in No. 3 of the journal *Creative Intelligence*.

volitional or conative. *And* it is essentially numinous.' (*Journal of the Society for Psychical Research*, 1972, vol. 46, p. 76.)

The concept of the Absolute as consciousness seems to me quite extraordinarily illuminating. Yet by itself it remains only a concept among others. Its real justification lies, not in any of the arguments I have discussed so far, but in the existence of the state of pure awareness itself. It is, I think, experience of this state which has led people to postulate an Absolute, or at least to identify the Absolute with consciousness.

However, 'experience' is not quite the right word. If we analyse people's attempts to describe what happens when they come to the state of pure awareness we find a rather strange feature common to nearly all the accounts. Instead of saying they 'experienced' pure awareness—which would imply a duality of experiencer and object of experience—people tend to say that they *became* the pure awareness, which they often describe as a 'Self'. This is well brought out in the passage by Symonds which I quoted on p. 49.

Perhaps an analogy may help to clarify what seems to happen on these occasions. Compare the individual awareness to a wave on the ocean. During meditation (or, less often, spontaneously) the activity of the nervous system and mind are progressively reduced. Eventually the activity ceases entirely; and now the wave that was the individual mind has disappeared, leaving only the calm ocean. We can say that the wave has become one with the ocean.

Now the question is, does the occurrence of a state of pure awareness justify the statement that this merging of the individual into the infinite has really occurred? Is the 'merging' perhaps a mere poetical conceit, the experience being fully explicable in terms of individual psychology?

One can certainly cite a great many passages which go to show that most people who have had this experience have believed that it did in fact consist in union with something or someone larger than themselves. There are of course exceptions. The orthodox of the great theistic religions have always maintained that this merging is indeed an illusion, and both Moslem and Christian writers have devoted a good deal of paper and ink to scotching the heresy that pure union is attainable. Even those who experienced the state and at first believed it consisted in union have sometimes had second thoughts—often for good reasons, since the orthodox have at times had recourse to more forceful methods of persuasion than mere literature.

The case of Martin Buber is interesting in this regard. Buber had an 'unforgettable experience' which at first led him to believe that he had 'attained to a union with the primal being or the godhead'. Subsequent reflection, however, caused him to change his mind. He had, he now believed, reached, not the 'soul of the All', but only the 'basic unity of my own soul . . . not in the least beyond individuation'. (*Between Man and Man*, London, p. 24.)

However, such an attitude to the experience is the exception rather than the rule; and in general I think it is fair to say that the experience itself tends naturally to produce a conviction that union has occurred; and if this interpretation is subsequently rejected it is because of conflict with a previously accepted 'over-belief'.

But of course the existence of a widespread belief in union does not prove anything. Even if almost everyone had the experience (as presumably would be the case if everyone practised meditation), this would not help; public verifiability, or even unanimity, is not by itself sufficient to constitute the criterion of objectivity.

It is certainly possible to put forward philosophical arguments to support what might be called the unitive theory. The fullest and best attempt to do this from the standpoint of a Western philosopher which is known to me is that of Stace (*MP*, pp. 134 et seq.). Valuable and important though Stace's arguments are, however, I do not think that they are fully conclusive. Moreover, I believe that, in the nature of the case, no fully conclusive arguments can be advanced.

This is not only because the topic is so contentious that one cannot hope to reach a final and irrefutable proof; the trouble lies deeper. When one discusses the nature of the Self one is using language, the tool of the 'relative' intellect, to reason about the absolute Self, which is the very source of reason. And this is ultimately an impossible task, for 'How can the Knower be known?'

I shall return to this theme in the next chapter, but here I should like to emphasize that I do not think we can expect philosophical arguments to do more than show the unitive theory to be a reasonable one. To go further one must put aside books and experiment for oneself.

The implication of all this is that discussion about whether the state of pure awareness should be regarded as subjective or objective is misconceived, since pure awareness is logically prior to both. Subjective and objective forms of knowledge are both concerned with the 'relative' world, and so they are modifications of, or superimposed on, that underlying reality of pure awareness which is absolute.

This is to restate in other terms the idea which I tried to convey by the cinema analogy at the end of Chapter II. Just as the relative states of awareness—waking, dreaming, deep sleep—depend for their existence upon the fourth state, pure awareness, so subjective and objective forms of knowledge are founded on, and united in, pure awareness, which is the Self.

This is the real reason why one cannot accurately speak of *experiencing* the state of pure awareness. It is better to say that one *reaches* the state, but even this is misleading for in reality— as the old Zen masters so often proclaimed—one is there already! Self-realization, Maharishi has frequently pointed out, is not a matter of doing anything or achieving anything but consists simply in recognizing what has always been the case. It is difficult to avoid using words like experience, reaching, becoming, without getting bogged down in clumsy circumlocutions, but at least one should recognize their inadequacy.

It is in relation to the identity of the individual self with the Cosmic Self that one should understand those extraordinarily moving verses (II, 16–23) of the Bhagavad Gita which deal with the immortality of the inner Being.

'Know That to be indeed indestructible by which all this is pervaded. None can work the destruction of this immutable Being.' (II, 17.)

Maharishi comments on this as follows:

'It may be clear here that the omnipresent Being and the spirit within man are not two different entities. They are found to be different because of the different individual nervous

92

systems. As the same sun appears as different when shining on different media, such as water and oil, so the same omnipresent Being, shining through different nervous systems, appears as different and forms the spirit, the subjective aspect of man's personality. When the nervous system is pure, Being reflects more and the spirit is more powerful, the mind more effective. When the nervous system is at its purest, then Being reflects in all its fullness, and the inner individuality of the spirit gains the level of unlimited eternal Being. Thus it is clear that in its essential nature the spirit is undying and omnipresent. This explains the universality of individuality.'

The English word 'spirit' has to do duty for the self in both its individualized and its universal aspects. Sanskrit uses two terms to describe the self, *Jiva* and *Atman*. Maharishi explains them thus:

'Jiva . . . is individualized cosmic existence; it is the individual spirit within the body. With its limitations removed, jiva is Atman, transcendent Being. . . .

'As the individual jiva in its essence is Atman, it is . . . called "eternal, imperishable, infinite".' (II, 18, Commentary.)

Yet even if one accepts that in the state of pure awareness people become united with a universal self, this still appears to leave unexplained the relation of this universal self to the phenomenal world. It might indeed seem that the mind-body problem has simply recurred on a much vaster scale. However, at this point one encounters another aspect of the Absolute which, like the universal self, is frequently found in descriptions of this kind of experience. This other aspect is the Being, or *sat*, attribute of the Absolute.

The consciousness, or *chit*, aspect of the Absolute, which we have been looking at so far, might be thought of as the Absolute manifesting itself on the subjective level. The counterpart of this on the objective level is the Being aspect.

The Absolute is said to be Being in the sense that it is the source of everything that exists. The analogy that Maharishi often uses is that of water, which can occur as vapour, liquid, or solid but is always the same compound of hydrogen and oxygen. In a rather similar way everything in the cosmos—stars, planets, rocks, plants, animals, man—is nothing but manifest Absolute. This statement is meant in two ways.

First, it is historical, in that manifestation is thought of as having occurred at some remote time in the past to give the universe as we know it today. Indian cosmology sees the evolution of the universe as a cyclical process, with a beginning and an end; moreover, the cycle is believed to repeat itself indefinitely. The resemblance of this scheme to the currently fashionable oscillating universe model is interesting, and indeed it is said that the oscillation period calculated for this model corresponds quite closely to the duration of the universe as given in the ancient Indian texts. We shall have to await further progress in cosmology to discover whether the ancient seers really did show such amazing prescience as these apparent resemblances suggest.

What is of more practical relevance today is the second way in which manifestation of the Absolute is conceived—as an ongoing process. According to this concept, the Absolute is manifesting itself continuously and dynamically, so that there is a continuous outflow of the energy which is the power that keeps everything going.

Again, the concepts of the Absolute as Being implies that every object, no matter how humble, contains within itself all degrees of manifestation, from the 'grossest' (most material) to the very subtlest *and beyond*—to the unmanifest Absolute itself, which is all-pervading and omnipresent—'greater than the greatest and smaller than the smallest', as the Upanishads put it.

This idea can be approached from two angles: intellectually and on the level of experience.

From the point of view of the intellect, quite a lot of the structure of reality has already been revealed by physics. Modern investigations into the nature of matter have revealed ever more subtle aspects—molecules, atoms, sub-atomic particles—until, as Koestler has put it, 'matter seems to dissolve into tensions in space'. Beyond this point, beyond the subtlest aspect of the relative world, lies . . . what? Nothing? Or the source of all that exists?

Perhaps physics can never answer this question. On the level of direct experience, however, it seems that the outflowing of energy from the Absolute can be discerned. Notice that I am not talking about belief, but about direct perception. What is at issue is not whether the 'mystics' *believe* that the Absolute gives rise to the world—of that there is no doubt—but whether they *perceive* it to do so. Many of them do in fact make this claim. Aurobindo, for example, says: 'Those who have thus possessed the Calm within can perceive always welling out from its silence the perennial supply of the energies that work in the universe.' (*The Life Divine*, Pondicherry, p. 33.) But the ability to perceive this fully requires development even beyond the stage of cosmic consciousness, as I shall discuss in the next chapter.

In conclusion, I would like to recapitulate the steps of evolution in awareness which I have considered so far. I started by pointing out that we ordinarily pass our lives in the three 'relative' states of waking, dreaming, and dreamless sleep. These three states are in reality modifications of a single undifferentiated 'ground' state which I called pure awareness. Pure awareness is the *fourth* state, and could be described as the underlying reality of the other three. It can be revealed by allowing the activity of the nervous system to slow down and stop, so that the projection of the three relative states upon the fourth state ceases temporarily.

At first the fourth state is gained only intermittently, that is, during meditation. Eventually, however, when it has been reached sufficiently often, it can be maintained spontaneously *along with* the three relative states. It is then never lost, whether one is awake or asleep, and this condition is called the *fifth* state, cosmic consciousness.

In each of these states one's perception of reality differs. Thus in the deep sleep state one has little or no knowledge of anything; in the dreaming state one has a hallucinatory knowledge of reality; and in the waking state one has a reasonably accurate knowledge of the 'grosser' features of existence.

In the fourth state one has a complete knowledge *of the Self alone*; everything which is not Self has ceased to exist. One thus has true knowledge, but of a very special kind.

In the fifth state one has once more knowledge of the external world, as in the ordinary waking state, but in addition there is the Self-awareness of the fourth state. Cosmic consciousness is thus a state of greatly enhanced knowledge of reality. Yet it is still incomplete because the relation between the Self and the outer world is not perceived.

This is a most important point. On one level this apparent gulf turns up as the free-will paradox, which I have already discussed. On another, it appears as the Absolute-relative paradox. This paradox can be stated quite simply: the Absolute is said to give rise to the relative world by a process of self-differentiation, and yet the Absolute has nothing to do with the world and *nothing happens to it at all.*

This paradox, which is sometimes debated by theologians and philosophers, is, according to Maharishi, a directly experienced reality of life in cosmic consciousness. Cosmic consciousness therefore reveals a basic contradiction in the nature of reality which, in the ordinary waking state, is obscured and only detectable by intellectual analysis.

Yet that is not the end of the story. On Maharishi's scheme further development of awareness is possible, and in the next chapter I shall try to show how this occurs. In doing so I shall, I hope, be able to shed a little light on some fascinating but usually obscure terrain.

# CHAPTER VII

## *The Seven States of Consciousness*

I HAVE NOW to consider Maharishi's sixth and seventh states of consciousness, and to show how these relate to the five which I have already discussed. It may well seem that after cosmic consciousness no further development is possible, and indeed so far as the subjective aspect of life is concerned this is true. However, perception of the world—the objective aspect—is still theoretically untouched. ('Theoretically', because the neat differentiation into stages which I am describing is in part a convenient fiction: much overlapping occurs, so that one may have flashes of a 'higher' state long before the previous one is fully established.)

To explain how refinement of objective perception occurs, let me recall the stages by which cosmic consciousness develops. The process of transcending consists in allowing the attention to travel systematically from the grossest aspect of the mind to the subtlest and then beyond, into the region of the unmanifest Absolute. Through continued repetition of this process one eventually gains complete familiarity with all the subjective aspects of creation, and this is cosmic consciousness. From this point on, further development consists in refinement of the mechanism of *perception* so that subtler values of the *objects of sense* come into awareness.

In discussing the Absolute as Being, I pointed out that the scheme presupposed the existence within every object of the full range of manifestation, down to the very subtlest and including the unmanifest Absolute itself. Enlightenment cannot be said to be complete until all levels of reality, from the grossest to subtlest and beyond, to all-pervading Absolute, are perceived. The process of gaining further enlightenment after cosmic consciousness repeats the sequence of events which led up to cosmic consciousness, but this time in terms of perception of the world. The process of transcending and gaining pure awareness consisted in the experiencing of progressively subtler grades of thought until the subtlest level was transcended and only pure awareness was left. Similarly, on the objective level, subtler and subtler aspects of the objects of perception are appreciated, until ultimately the subtlest are transcended and the omnipresent Absolute is reached.

To the state in which the subtlest relative level of the objects of sense is appreciated Maharishi gives the name 'God consciousness'. This is the *sixth* state of consciousness.

Like 'meditation', the word 'God' can give rise to misunderstanding. Maharishi is not talking about God as an object of belief, or even, primarily, of worship; he is saying that to someone whose awareness has reached this state the world is 'glorified' and takes on a personal quality. In the Bhagavad Gita the Lord says: 'He who sees Me everywhere, and sees everything in Me, I am not lost to him nor is He lost to Me.' (VI, 30.) On this verse Maharishi comments: '. . . when the fullness of Being overflows through the mind into the fields of perception, when spiritual Unity prevails even on the level of the senses, when the oneness of God overtakes life, then is that state attained where perception of anything whatsoever is perception of the Being made manifest. Then his consciousness finds a direct relationship with the Lord, with Being made manifest, who becomes a living Reality for him on that supremely divine level of consciousness. Then he and his Lord are not lost to one another.'

In this passage there has been a striking change in tone. Instead of, as hitherto, speaking of the Absolute as impersonal, Maharishi is now identifying it with the Personal Lord. This may be a startling and even unwelcome development to some people who have accepted the identification of the Self with the Absolute which I put forward in Chapter VI.[1] An impersonal Absolute is one thing, a personal God quite another. For most of us today,

---

[1] I must confess that it was so at first for me. Having, as I explained in the Introduction, gone to a good deal of trouble to rid myself of the beliefs of a conventional religious upbringing, I found it rather hard to be expected to swallow them all once more. However, as my understanding of Maharishi's ideas began to grow a little, I saw that I had really been making a fuss about nothing. It was an extraordinary experience to see ideas I had rejected as meaningless—because they had been taught by people who did not themselves fully understand them—suddenly catch fire, like diamonds in a muddy stream.

a God who sits in heaven recording our sins of commission and omission and assigning praise and blame—Tennyson's 'infinite clergyman', in fact—is no more credible than the gods of Olympus. Of course, this is not the conception which Maharishi is proposing.

What he is saying is that, for people at a certain level of awareness, the world is suffused with the light of Being, which in this state is seen to be personal. This is not a question of belief, but simply of perception. It depends, in fact, upon the physiological condition of one's nervous system.

God consciousness is a logical development of cosmic consciousness. Cosmic consciousness is permanent awareness of the Absolute on the subjective level. Now the Absolute does have features on account of which it could reasonably be called 'God'. First, it is consciousness itself, and in this sense is alive. Second, union with it is described as transcendental bliss—the peace that passes all understanding. Third, it arouses feelings of the holy and the sacred. Fourth, it is the source of all values and all goodness. (I shall have more to say about this later.) Fifth, it differentiates itself into the phenomenal world by its own power—not as a temporal but as a timeless and eternal activity.

What happens in God consciousness, Maharishi says, is that these qualities of the Absolute, which in cosmic consciousness were confined to the subjective level, now begin to overflow into the world at large. Thus the world, as well as the Self, is seen to be filled with the Divine. It is not that the world becomes suddenly liable to the caprices of a personal God; the world remains governed by natural laws, but these laws in their working now appear as personal and divine.

Someone who, like myself, is not anywhere near this level of awareness obviously cannot say much about it. However, many 'ordinary' people appear to have had flashes of God consciousness and have left descriptions of what they experienced. Here, for example, is a well-known passage from R. M. Bucke, which I think embodies many of the most characteristic features:

'I had spent the evening in a great city, with two friends, reading and discussing poetry and philosophy. We parted at midnight. I had a long drive in a hansom to my lodging. My mind, deeply under the influence of the ideas, images, and emotions called up by the reading and talk, was calm and peaceful. I was in a state of quiet, almost passive enjoyment, not actually thinking, but letting ideas, images, and emotions flow of themselves, as it were, through my mind. All at once, without warning of any kind, I found myself wrapped in a flame-coloured cloud. For an instant I thought of fire, a great conflagration somewhere close by in that great city; the next, I knew that the fire was within myself. Directly afterwards there came upon me a sense of exultation, of immense joyousness accompanied or immediately followed by an intellectual illumination impossible to describe. Among other things, I did not merely come to believe, but I saw that the universe is not composed of dead matter but is, on the contrary, a living Presence; I became conscious in myself of eternal life. It was not a conviction that I would have eternal life, but a consciousness that I possessed eternal life then; I saw that all men are immortal; that the cosmic order is such that without any peradventure all things work together for the good of each and all; that the foundation principle of the world, of all the worlds, is what we call love, and that the happiness of each and all is in the long run absolutely certain. The vision lasted a few seconds and was gone, but the memory of it and the sense of the reality of what it taught has remained during the quarter of a century which has since elapsed. I knew that what the vision showed was true. I had attained to a point of view from which I saw that it must be true. That view, that conviction, I may say that consciousness, has never, even during periods of the deepest depression, been lost.' (Quoted in James, *VRE*, p. 385.)

Notice particularly the phrase 'a living Presence'. This is the hallmark of God consciousness; the world is seen to have come alive. Notice, too, the 'immense joyousness'; Maharishi compares cosmic consciousness to seeing the world through ordinary glasses and God consciousness to seeing it through golden glasses.[1] (This should not be taken to mean that God consciousness is an illusion; the golden glasses simply reveal qualities in

---

[1] Incidentally, notice too the circumstances of this experience. Bucke's mind was 'calm and peaceful', and he was 'not actually thinking, but letting ideas, images, and emotions flow of themselves'. In short, he was ripe to 'transcend'.

the world which were always there.) The personal God is experienced directly by the senses when these are sensitive enough to register the subtlest relative levels. Bucke says 'I did not merely come to *believe*, but I *saw* that the universe . . . is a living Presence.' (My italics.) The difference between seeing and believing is vital. Belief in God, or lack of belief, is unimportant; what matters is direct experience.

Thus, we now have two apparently quite separate ways of thinking about God. On the one hand God can be conceived of as impersonal, eternal, unchanging, without qualities—in a word, Absolute. This is the aspect of God which is cognized in transcendental consciousness and in cosmic consciousness. Under this aspect God is referred to as 'It'. On the other hand, God can also be conceived of as personal, with qualities, and in this case is referred to, not as It, but as He or She (or even, as in some androgynous Indian versions, as both He and She). (For Maharishi's own description of the impersonal and personal aspects of God, see *SBAL*, pp. 271–9.)

Can these two versions of God be reconciled? Maharishi's answer is that they cannot be reconciled intellectually but that at a certain level of experience there ceases to be any contradiction between them. The way out of the impasse consists in deepening one's awareness.

Let us see how, according to Maharishi, this resolution occurs. The essential nature of reality is, as we have seen, that everything consists of manifest Absolute. After God consciousness has been lived for some time, perception becomes still subtler, to include, not only the subtlest relative, but also the omnipresent Absolute. 'As the Union grows more complete, the link of worship, of adoration and devotion, finds fulfilment in its own extinction, leaving worshipper and worshipped together in perfect oneness, in the oneness of absolute Unity. Then he and his God are one in himself. Then himself has become Himself; his vision is in terms of Himself, his pleasure and pain are in terms of Himself.' (*BG*, VI, 32, commentary.)

The state described in this passage is the logical culmination of God consciousness. It is the *seventh* state of consciousness, which Maharishi calls *Unity*. It represents the highest state which the human nervous system is capable of reaching.

Descriptions of Unity undoubtedly sound strange. This is because our language is adapted to frame either–or statements. We can say that things are many, or that they are one, but what the mystic—the man in Unity—perceives is that they are *both* many *and* one. This cannot be expressed in words without contradiction. For Maharishi, however, everything depends on the level of one's awareness—which in turn depends on the physical state of one's nervous system. 'Philosophers call this a mystical[1] experience, but it is no more mysterious than is the working of a clock for a child. On one level of consciousness it is normal, on another it is mysterious, and again on another it is impossible.' (*BG*, VI, 30, commentary.)

Maharishi's claim is that statements which, on the level of 'ignorance', sound paradoxical are clear and straightforward to someone who has raised his level of awareness to the requisite degree by the practice of transcendental meditation. *Unity is the state which resolves the Absolute-relative paradox.* The man in Unity sees both aspects of life—ever-changing relative, unchanging Absolute—simultaneously, and sees that they are one. As the Upanishads say, 'all this is Brahman.' Precisely the same insight is expressed in two passages from Eckhart: 'All that a man has externally in multiplicity is intrinsically One. Here all blades of grass, wood and stone, all things are

---

[1] Maharishi has always disliked the word 'mysticism'. In this he resembles Abbot Chapman, who calls it 'hateful, modern, and ambiguous'. (*The Spiritual Letters of Dom John Chapman*, ed. Hudleston, Sheed & Ward, 1935, p. 297.) The reason is not hard to find; cognate as it is with 'mystery', it carries many unwanted associations.

Thus the *Shorter Oxford English Dictionary* has: 'As a term of reproach. a. Applied loosely to any religious belief associated with self-delusion and dreamy confusion of thought. b. Sometimes applied to philosophical or scientific theories which assume occult qualities or mysterious agencies of which no rational account can be given.' Certainly one cannot be surprised that for most people today 'mysticism' is a term of abuse. And—give a dog a bad name—this unfortunate aura of humbug has probably helped to prevent the subject from receiving all the philosophical and scientific attention it deserves.

Now, if I have at all succeeded in my intention so far, I have at least shown that Maharishi, far from favouring confusion, dreaminess, or the occult, is concerned to clear up the confusions by which the subject has for so long been obscured. I should, therefore, prefer to avoid using the word 'mysticism' altogether, but I think it is prescribed by custom. From now on, therefore, I shall use it when necessary; but I do so with the warning that I am restricting its application to what the *Shorter Oxford English Dictionary* calls, elsewhere in its definition, 'union with the Divine nature'—in a word, yoga (literally, 'yoking'). This excludes such phenomena as the hearing of voices and seeing of visions.

One. This is the deepest depth and thereby am I completely captivated.' And again: 'Say Lord, when is a man in mere understanding? I say to you "when a man sees one thing separated from another." And when is he above mere understanding? That I can tell you: "When he sees all in all, then a man stands above mere understanding." ' (Quoted R. Otto, *Mysticism East and West*, Macmillan, pp. 61 and 45.)

It is interesting to compare these two quotations with the Bhagavad Gita: 'In a brahmin endowed with learning and humility, in a cow, in an elephant, in a dog and even in one who has lost his caste, the enlightened perceive the same.' (V, 18.)

On this verse Maharishi makes the following comment. 'This does not mean that such a man fails to see a cow or is unable to distinguish it from a dog. Certainly he sees a cow as a cow and a dog as a dog, but the form of the cow and the form of the dog fail to blind him to the oneness of the Self, which is the same in both . . . The enlightened man, while beholding and acting in the whole of diversified creation, does not fall from his steadfast Unity of life, with which his mind is saturated and which remains indelibly infused in his vision.'

Thus for Maharishi, as for Eckhart, the 'deepest depth' consists in seeing both the oneness of the Absolute and the multiplicity of the world *simultaneously*. It is in this sense that the Absolute-relative paradox is resolved. But of course it is resolved only on the level of perception; as soon as the resolution is expressed in words the paradox reappears.

It seems to be this essential paradoxicality which has given rise to the alleged ineffability of mystical experience. There has been much discussion about the reasons for this ineffability which, according to William James and others, is a cardinal feature of mysticism. A number of theories, which Stace summarizes (*MP*, pp. 280 et seq.), have been put forward; the one I myself prefer is that the difficulty arises *because descriptions of the mystical experience are essentially self-contradictory*.

I think that this theory is in general supported by the world's mystical literature. One interesting implication of the argument is that the mystical experience is not really ineffable; the mystics do frequently describe it very well. The difficulty they encounter is actually psychological. As rational men, they find themselves forced to use self-contradictory language which cannot be squared with the ordinary rules of logic.

The solution to the mystics' difficulty is to recognize that mystical experience is a-logical. Logic belongs to the relative world; it can gain no foothold in the Absolute, which is beyond the distinctions with which logic deals. The very greatest mystical utterances, such as the Upanishads, are in no way inhibited by the psychological difficulty of stating the mystical paradox; indeed, they proclaim it triumphantly. But this is unusual; most religious texts, being at a lesser degree of profundity, tend to emphasize one aspect of the paradox at the expense of the other.

It is for this reason that some mystics appear to support a dualistic interpretation, others a monistic one. Cultural forces are undoubtedly important here; mystics brought up in the Judaeo-Christian religions tend to favour the duality aspect of the paradox, and to conceive of God as transcendent and Other. Union with God they regard as heresy, and the duality of worshipped and worshipper is insisted upon. Indian religion, on the contrary, has leaned towards the Absolute side of the paradox, and more often thinks of God as the Self, the inner Being. But the two approaches overlap a good deal; there are theistic trends in India, monistic ones in the West.

However, this is not the whole story. One should be wary of imagining that all the mystics are saying the same thing, and that the differences in the various world religions are simply due to dull-minded legalists who distort the mystics' pro-nouncements to fit preconceived dogmas. It seems much more likely that dogma usually derives from mystical experience than the other way round.

On Maharishi's scheme, we can easily see why there should be differences in the teachings of different mystics. Everything will depend on the level of experience of the particular mystic. In India, for example, whole schools (Samkhya, Yoga, Jaina) teach that the end of enlightenment is the discovery of the individual pure ego, which is not thought of as a larger Self. (This is exactly Buber's position.) Presumably such doctrines are based on experience as far as transcendental consciousness but not beyond.

To this extent, then, I must disagree with those who claim that mystical experience is always and everywhere the same. However, this is not to say that the mystics of the theistic religions, especially Christianity, enjoy a type of experience which is not vouchsafed to Hindus, Buddhists, and the like. Claims for the uniqueness of Christian mystical experience are sometimes made, especially by Catholics (see, for example, R. C. Zaehner's *Mysticism Sacred and Profane*, Oxford, 1957). I therefore find the Catholic Abbot Chapman's remarks on St John of the Cross to be of quite exceptional importance. Chapman was not only a scholar; by all accounts he was also one of the greatest 'spiritual directors' of modern times. He therefore speaks with a great deal of authority on both the theoretical and the practical level. Yet he seems to have been puzzled until the end of his life by the relation between 'contemplative prayer' (meditation, in my terminology) and Christocentric devotion. He could find nothing specifically Christian in the mystical experience: '... the problem of *reconciling* mysticism with Christianity is ... more difficult ... St John of the Cross is like a sponge full of Christianity. You can squeeze it all out, and the full mystical theory remains. Consequently for fifteen years or so I hated St John of the Cross and called him a Buddhist ... Then I found I had wasted fifteen years, so far as prayer was concerned!' (*SL*, p. 269.)

And now here is quite a different witness—a rationalist. Marghanita Laski made, in her original and important study *Ecstasy*, a detailed examination of material derived not only from published 'literary' and 'religious' texts but also from a questionnaire answered by sixty-three of her friends and acquaintances. On the basis of this unusually practical investigation, she concludes that 'No variety of ecstatic experience that appears in my texts is available exclusively to Christians; to name an experience a Christian one is to name it according to its over-belief and not according to its kind.' (*Ecstasy*, Cresset, 1961, p. 372.)

Maharishi's scheme suggests that at least four types of mystical experience should be distinguishable, related respectively to transcendental consciousness, cosmic consciousness, God consciousness, and Unity. And in fact many writers on mysticism do describe these states under various names. Stace, for example, divides mystical experience into 'introvertive' and 'extrovertive' types; the introvertive I should call transcendental consciousness, and the extrovertive would be Maharishi's other three states (cosmic consciousness, God consciousness, and Unity) lumped together. Miss Laski also has this division into introvertive and extrovertive experiences, which she calls 'withdrawal' and 'intensity' respectively. She has relatively little to say about the first kind, and indeed she admits that she could not learn much about it; in this she differs from Stace, who makes the introvertive experience the key to mysticism. However, she arranges 'intensity' experiences into three groups in ascending order of value, and these correspond fairly well to cosmic consciousness, God consciousness, and Unity.

It is interesting to see how an understanding of the seven states of consciousness can shed light on the Islamic theologian Ghazālī, who I suspect has misled even so erudite a scholar as Professor Zaehner. Ghazālī (1059–1111) was recognized as the greatest authority of his time on theology and law, but could find no spiritual satisfaction in either. He therefore abandoned his chair of divinity at Baghdad and spent the last sixteen years of his life in a quest for direct experience as a Sufi. His immense prestige was largely responsible for reconciling Sufism with Muslim orthodoxy, and his powerful intellect was devoted to analysing the mystical experience which it seems (though one cannot be sure) that he attained. Ghazālī has often been compared to St Augustine.[1]

It must be admitted that Ghazālī's writings, especially on the more esoteric aspects of Sufism, are frequently gnomic. However, it seems to me that there are remarkable similarities between some of his ideas and those which underly transcendental meditation.

Take first the actual Sufi meditation—*dhikr*. Zaehner says: '. . . in the last stage of the meditation on the name of God all disappears except the object of the meditation.' (*Hindu and Muslim Mysticism*, Athlone, 1960, p. 167.) This, as Zaehner

[1] On the importance of Ghazālī for Sufism, see Arberry, *Sufism*, Allen & Unwin, 1950, pp. 79–83.

himself points out (ibid., p. 168), is remarkably similar to the meditation described in the sixth chapter of the Bhagavad Gita.

Here, in fact, Ghazālī is referring to the transcendental state. But this is only the beginning. Ghazālī, Zaehner says disapprovingly, 'succeeds in combining a rigid monism with a full-blooded pantheism.' (Ibid., p. 168.) After the transcendental state, Ghazālī says, yet higher states develop: 'When he [sc. the Sufi] has reached this stage . . . the form of the spiritual world (*malakūt*) begins to reveal itself to him and the souls of angels and prophets begin to appear in comely forms, and that which is willed by his Divine Majesty begins to show forth. Grand mystic states appear which it is impossible to describe.' (Quoted ibid., p. 169.)

This passage excites Zaehner's strongest disapproval. 'This, surely, is downright frivolous. Here is a man with a world-wide reputation as a philosopher, who after making the tremendous claim that he has, in some sense, *been* God, is conscious of no bathos in referring to visions of lesser beings as if this were yet a deeper plunge into the unseen. In the Indian tradition which can claim rather more expertise in these matters than Ghazālī visions of this kind are regarded as being premonitory signs that *precede* the vision of the 'self' or the achievement of isolation: they are ancillary to the achievement of oneness and of no value in themselves.' (Ibid., p. 169.)

If Ghazālī is really referring to visions during meditation Zaehner is of course perfectly correct in his strictures. I suspect, however, that Ghazālī, in his admittedly flowery language, is actually talking about God consciousness. The higher mystic states, he says, *follow* the gaining of Self-awareness, and they consist in seeing the divine will in action.

In other passages Ghazālī apparently speaks of Unity. 'If you ever see anyone at peace . . . you will understand [him] only when all of you passes away in him, and all becomes his glory, so that duality ceases and unity appears. He remains, and you do not; or he passes away in you, and you remain and he does not. Or else both of you pass away in God and pay no attention to yourselves, and that is perfection. From this oneness there is perfect repose. In short, so long as duality persists, no repose is possible for repose is [only] in unity and oneness.' (Quoted ibid., p. 170.)

I do not wish to build too much on these passages. To me, however, they suggest that the Sufis of Ghazāli's time recognized that progression from inner to outer Unity which is at the heart of Maharishi's concept of spiritual evolution.

My conclusion is that it is the *uniting* of monism and theism, and not a one-sided insistence on either, that is the real message of the mystics. Here I find myself wholly in agreement with Stace, who puts forward a definition of pantheism which encompasses both ways of interpreting mystical experience:

'According to the definition which I propose, pantheism is the philosophy which asserts together both of the following propositions, namely:

1. The world is identical with God.
2. The world is distinct from, that is to say, *not* identical with God.

'I am of the opinion that paradoxicality is one of the universal characteristics of all mysticism. This basic paradoxicality will of course be reflected in all philosophies which are, so to speak, high-level interpretations of mysticism. And because pantheism, however much it may wear the outward garb of logic and rationalism, as in Spinoza, always has its roots in mysticism, we shall expect it to be paradoxical. Only those critics who are deceived by Spinoza's superficial geometrical method, and who are unable to penetrate below the surface to the subterranean springs of Spinoza's thought, will believe otherwise. The proposition that the world is both identical with, and different from, God, may be called the pantheistic paradox.' (*MP*, p. 212.)

This paradox is certainly a feature of Maharishi's teaching, as I have already pointed out. And I believe that we must accept it, without trying to get round it or argue it away, if we are to render unto Caesar the things that are Caesar's and unto God the things that are God's. Take, for example, the question of *maya*. Some writers on Indian philosophy adopt the view that the doctrine of maya implies that the world is an illusion. But Maharishi rejects this view. Maya, he says, means literally 'that which is not'; however it refers, not to the world, but to the connection between the world and the Absolute. The Absolute manifests itself as the world, yet remains quite separate from it. This—the essential mystical paradox—is, according to Maharishi, the true meaning of maya.

It is vital to realize that although the theory of the mystical paradox can be extracted from the writings of the mystics, for the mystics themselves it is not a theory but a direct account of the experience which, in its fullest development, is what Maharishi calls the state of Unity.

The paradoxical conception of God to which such experience gives rise is well expressed by Ruysbroeck: 'Tranquillity according to His Essence, activity according to His nature: absolute repose, absolute fecundity . . . The Divine Persons who form one sole God are in the fecundity of their nature ever active; and in the simplicity of their essence they form the Godhead . . . Thus God according to the Persons is Eternal Work; but according to the essence and its perpetual stillness, he is Eternal Rest.' (Quoted Evelyn Underhill, *Mysticism*, pp. 434–5.)

Exactly the same paradox is the characteristic teaching of the Upanishads, as appears in this passage from the Isa Upanishad: 'The Spirit, without moving, is swifter than the mind . . . Standing still, he overtakes those who run . . . He moves, and he moves not.'

At this point a full turn of the spiral has been completed. The Absolute-relative paradox has gone through all its phases. At the end of the last chapter I traced the paradox from the state of ignorance, in which it was latent, detectable only by intellectual analysis in such forms as the mind-matter and free-will problems, to cosmic consciousness, where it became evident on the perceptual level as the basis of all experience. I also said that further development would bring about resolution of the paradox, and now we are able to see what this means. Resolution begins in God consciousness and is complete in Unity.

It is this resolution which constitutes full 'enlightenment'. When I said, in the Introduction, that enlightenment offered a standpoint from which ultimate truth could be discerned, this

## THE SEVEN STATES OF CONSCIOUSNESS

| State | Awareness of Self | Awareness of Outer World | Absolute-relative Paradox |
|---|---|---|---|
| 1. Dreamless Sleep  } 'Relative' States | Absent | Absent | — |
| 2. Dreaming | Absent | Hallucinatory | — |
| 3. Waking | Absent | Present | Discoverable by intellect |
| 4. Transcendental Consciousness | Present | Absent | Absent |
| 5. Cosmic Consciousness | Present | Present | Present to perception |
| 6. God Consciousness | Present | Present | Partially resolved |
| 7. Unity | Present | Present | Resolved |

was what I meant. In Indian thought, there is no absolute truth except on the level of the Absolute; all other truth is relative, and depends on one's state of awareness. Thus the truth of the dreaming state differs from that of the waking state, and the truth of the state of 'ignorance' differs from that of the state of cosmic consciousness. The traditional problems of philosophy—mind versus matter, free will versus determinism, and so on—are insoluble on the level of logical analysis, but at the level of Unity they no longer appear as problems.

The seven states of consciousness constitute a conceptual scheme which has, I believe, great explanatory power in all kinds of fields, scientific, philosophical and religious. In the following chapters I shall be assuming the validity of the scheme and applying it to a number of problems concerned with awareness and its transformations which happen to interest me; but I am under no illusion that I can do more than scratch their surface. I hope to be able to return to some of them at greater length in a later book.

I have tried to summarize the chief features of the seven states in the form of a table which will, I hope, help to clarify their inter-relations.

# CHAPTER VIII

## *Some Rival Interpretations*

IN THE LAST chapter I concluded that Maharishi's seven states of consciousness provided a framework within which mystical phenomena could be accommodated. The underlying assumption, however, was that there is something to be accounted for; in other words, that mystical experience does bring us, as Broad supposes, into contact with some 'Reality'.[1] Now I have to examine the possibility that mystical experience can be adequately explained in purely psychological terms. If this is true it will, of course, render much mystical theory otiose.

It is a commonly held idea today that psychology has satisfactorily 'explained' mysticism. So I think the first point that is worth making is the extraordinary variability in the alleged explanations. Marghanita Laski remarks that, in a BBC television discussion on mysticism, 'one speaker assumed that the states discussed were caused by God, another by manic-depression, a third by schizophrenia, while a fourth said the power concerned was the collective unconscious which inspires poets and saints but goes sour in mental patients.' (*Ecstasy*, p. 168.) Where so many explanations are proffered (and of course the list I have just cited is by no means exhaustive) we may be forgiven for doubting whether any of them is likely to be right.

Psychological explanations of mysticism fall into two broad categories. On the one hand there are those which attribute

---

[1] 'I am prepared to admit that such experiences occur among people of different races and social conditions, and that they have occurred at all periods of history. I am prepared to admit that, although the experiences have differed considerably at different times and places, and although the interpretations of them have differed still more, there are probably certain characteristics which are common to them all and suffice to distinguish them from all other types of experience. In view of this I think it more likely than not that in religious and mystical experience men come into contact with some Reality or aspect of Reality which they do not come into contact with in any other way.' (C. D. Broad, *Religion, Philosophy, and Psychical Research*, Routledge & Kegan Paul, London, 1953, pp. 172–3.)

the experiences to some perturbation of normal function; on the other, those which are based on the supposition that these experiences serve a purpose. I shall start by considering the first group.

To illustrate the kind of case which is sometimes adduced as evidence for the truth of the contention that mystical experience is pathological, consider a recent paper by Kenneth Dewhurst and A. W. Beard entitled 'Sudden Religious Conversion in Temporal Lobe Epilepsy' (*British Journal of Psychiatry*, 1970, vol. 117, pp. 497–507). Temporal lobe epilepsy is an interesting disorder which can produce bizarre alterations in consciousness. As the name implies, it is a form of epileptic disturbance originating in the temporal lobe of the brain.

Epilepsy, as Dewhurst and Beard point out, has been associated with religiosity for over a hundred years. (May the ancient and widespread idea that epilepsy is a sacred disease be relevant here?) 'Mystical delusional experiences' are, they suggest, common in epilepsy. In their paper they report six patients showing these features. The most interesting was a man aged fifty-five who had worked as a bus driver until, after an epileptic attack, he had to change to being a conductor. The first conversion experience occurred as follows. 'In the middle of collecting fares, he was suddenly overcome with a feeling of bliss. He felt he was literally in Heaven. He collected the fares correctly, telling his passengers at the same time how pleased he was to be in Heaven. When he returned home he appeared not to recognize his wife, but she did get from him a somewhat incoherent account of his celestial experience. Later the patient told his G.P. that he felt as if a bomb had burst in his head and that he thought he was paddling in water. On admission to [hospital], he was constantly laughing to himself; he said that he had seen God and that his wife and family would soon join him in Heaven; his mood was elated, his thought disjointed and he readily admitted to hearing music and voices. . . . He remained in this state of exaltation, hearing divine and angelic voices, for two days. Afterwards he was able to recall these experiences and he continued to believe in their validity.'

For the next two years he remained religious; he then had three seizures on three successive days and became elated again. 'He stated that his mind had "cleared". (A letter to his wife, in which he attempted to express his religious ideas was, in fact, unintelligible.) During this episode he lost his faith. "I used to believe in Heaven and Hell, but after this experience I do not believe there is a hereafter." He also lost his belief in the divinity of Christ. . . . This sudden conversion was marked by an elevation of mood and a general sense of well-being and clarity of mind. He considered that this second episode also had the nature of a revelation.'

This patient's experiences do contain some elements reminiscent of mysticism, especially the feeling of bliss and the impression of new knowledge gained. But notice that these appeared in a general setting of mental disorder; the patient's letter was incomprehensible, his thought was disjointed, his behaviour obviously disordered. These features are still more evident in the other five patients discussed by Dewhurst and Beard. One, for example, said: 'I was not thanking God, I was with God. God isn't something hard looking down on us, God is trees and flowers and beauty and love.' This, so far as it goes, might be a description of God consciousness. But he goes on: '. . . God was telling me, at last you have found someone who can help you, and he was talking about you, doctor, He was talking about you. . . .' This experience led the patient to realize suddenly that he himself was the Son of God and could cure cancer; he had visions, and believed he could understand people's thoughts.

All these patients, in fact, had quite clear evidence of mental and physical pathology. Their thinking showed strong paranoid trends; they suffered from hallucinations and delusions, and their relationship to their family and the world at large suffered in consequence. It is scarcely justifiable to generalize these characteristics to mystics in general, and to infer that any insights which such people may have had are no more worthy of credence than the delusions of paranoia. Yet this seems to be the view of Dewhurst and Beard, who speculate that a number of well-known mystics, including St Paul, St Teresa of Avila, and St Thérèse of Lisieux, were epileptics. As they admit, this is impossible to prove. 'Unfortunately, the biographical details of several of these saints and mystics are too meagre to allow an accurate assessment of their experiences. There is, however, little doubt that some suffered from temporal lobe epilepsy causing states of altered awareness which brought about their sudden conversion.'

The approach of these authors is fairly typical of what William James called 'medical materialism'. 'Medical materialism finishes up Saint Paul by calling his vision on the road to Damascus a discharging lesion of the occipital cortex, he being an epileptic. It snuffs out Saint Teresa as an hysteric, Saint Francis of Assisi as an hereditary degenerate. George Fox's discontent with the shams of his age, and his pining for spiritual veracity, it treats as a symptom of a disordered colon. Carlyle's organtones of misery it accounts for by a gastroduodenal catarrh. . . . And medical materialism then thinks that the spiritual authority of all such personages is successfully undermined.' (*VRE*, p. 35.)

To my mind Dewhurst and Beard make the mistake of building too much on a group of severely abnormal patients. I believe we shall learn more by looking at the experiences of people who are normal, or nearly so, but who suffer transient disturbances of consciousness.

One disorder which is common in otherwise normal individuals is migraine. Like epilepsy, migraine can produce altered states of consciousness; indeed, many authorities believe that migraine and epilepsy are related. Both epileptic and migrainous attacks may be ushered in by an aura—that is, a sensory hallucination. In the case of migraine this is usually visual. In his recent book *Migraine* (Faber, pp. 112–15), Oliver W. Sacks discusses the visions of Hildegard of Bingen (1098–1180). Hildegard, 'a nun and mystic of exceptional intellectual and literary powers' (op. cit., p. 112), not only described her visions but also drew them. They are, Sacks says, 'indisputably migrainous' (ibid., p. 114). However, they were nonetheless 'instrumental in directing her towards a life of holiness and mysticism. They provide a unique example of the manner in which a physiological event, banal, hateful, or meaningless to the vast majority of people, can become, in a privileged consciousness, the substrate of a supreme ecstatic inspiration. One must go to Dostoievski, who experienced on occasion ecstatic epileptic auras to which he attached momentous significance, to find an adequate historical parallel.' (Ibid., p. 115.)

Sacks thus concedes that the visions had some pragmatic value; but one cannot suppose that Hildegard herself would have continued to enjoy them in the same way if she had known their true nature. This is the real point at issue. Hildegard's visions are not directly relevant to the question of mysticism, for I have already specifically excluded visual and auditory hallucinations from mystical experience (see p. 102n.), but they are relevant indirectly. If mystical experience proper is ultimately attributable to cerebral malfunction it will lose much of its importance, even if it can on occasion serve as a source of inspiration.

Some migrainous auras affect, not vision, but mood, and these have more relevance to mystical experience. Sacks lists the following features as characteristic:

1. Their sudden onset.
2. Their apparent sourcelessness, and frequent incongruity with the foreground contents of consciousness.
3. Their overwhelming quality.
4. A sense of passivity, and of the affect being 'forced' into the mind.
5. Their brief duration (they rarely last more than a few minutes).
6. The sense of stillness and timelessness they convey; such states may wax in depth or intensity, but this occurs despite the absence of any experiential 'happening'.
7. Their difficulty or impossibility of description.

Such states are not confined to migraine and epilepsy, but may occur in schizophrenia, fever, intoxication, hysteria, and other abnormal conditions. Furthermore, as Sacks remarks, 'We are inevitably reminded of William James' listing of the qualities of "mystical" states: ineffability, noetic quality, transiency passivity.' (Ibid., p. 92.)

Migrainous auras may also take on the quality of intense fear or, more rarely, awe or rapture. There may be prolonged and overwhelming intense experience of sudden familiarity (*déjà vu*) or the opposite (*jamais vu*), and such experiences may be associated with a great variety of other feelings: feelings that time has stopped, or is mysteriously recapitulating itself; feelings of intense nostalgia, sometimes combined with an uprush of forgotten memories; feelings of clairvoyance; or—and this is interesting—feelings that the world or oneself is new-minted. In all cases, Sacks says, there is a feeling that consciousness has been doubled.[1]

With these descriptions we are undoubtedly brought much nearer to something that sounds like mystical experience. W. Grey Walter, the neurophysiologist, seems to believe that mystical experience is indeed hallucinatory, and his discussion of this question in *The Neuro-physiological Aspects of Hallucinations and Illusory Experience* (Society for Psychical Research) is most illuminating. He describes the case of a patient 'who frequently saw a fair-sized green crocodile which gave off an unpleasant musty odour [and] was at first naturally terrified by the creature but, later, reconciled himself to its apparition with the reflection that of course by now it must be tame'. (Op. cit., p. 5.) Another patient 'had attacks preceded by a vision of an ugly old crone dressed in rags and—like the crocodile— emitting a disagreeable smell, who would clatter about in the kitchen, apparently cooking some unsavoury dish. He was alarmed by this recurrent vision which resembled the witch of a fairy tale, but as she seemed to mean no harm he accepted her as a familiar, and mentioned that—apart from her ragged clothes and odour—she rather resembled his grandmother.' (Ibid., pp. 5–6.)

As Grey Walter points out, what is remarkable about these elaborate hallucinations (which contain visual, auditory,

---

[1] Perhaps I might bring in a personal note here. I used myself to suffer from migraine (though the attacks had almost ceased before I began to meditate). I have on occasion experienced changes of mood of the sort described by Sacks and I can vouch for their strangeness. Certainly they bore no resemblance to any experiences I have had as a result of meditating; indeed, they were the very antithesis of such experiences. Whereas the migraine auras made me feel as if I were in some way changed and strange to myself, the effects of meditation have always been to make me feel more fully myself—more 'normal', or even 'ordinary', than before. There is a 'wholeness' about the experiences of transcendental meditation which is, for me at least, unique.

olfactory, and suitable emotional components) is the way in which they are projected quite naturally and completely into the general background of external reality. 'Illusory figures of this sort will often come through a doorway, sit on a chair, use an implement and yet be appreciated sooner or later as illusory or unreal. This of course distinguishes them from the delusions of the psychotic which presumably should be considered in another category, though, according to my hypothesis they too necessarily have a basis in cerebral mechanisms.' (Ibid., pp. 6–7.)

Grey Walter's hypothesis is that all such experiences can be explained on the basis of physical disturbances, in the widest sense, within the brain. As a rule such disturbances will produce random effects—blobs of light, unpleasant smells, *déjà vu*, and so on; and these are common even in normal people. The appearance of elaborate hallucinations like those of the crocodile and the old woman will depend on the occurrence of a complex brain disturbance 'slight enough to be compatible with normal function but so widespread as to involve at the same time a number of functional systems', which is 'as unlikely as being dealt a complete suit at bridge or a straight flush at poker'. The important point is that 'the illusion of experience will tend toward perfection as the complexity of the disturbances approximates to physiological activation'. In other words, if a disturbance pattern produces a brain state which is indistinguishable from that which would exist if the hallucinatory scene were real, the hallucination will in fact be indistinguishable from reality so far as the subject is concerned.

Notice that such hallucinations need not be confined to people with abnormal brains. About twenty per cent of normal people, if exposed to light flickering at a certain rate, show electrical brain rhythms similar to those occurring in epileptic fits, and some suffer actual fits. Organized hallucinations may occur in these circumstances, though they are rare. The implication, Grey Walter feels, is that liability to epilepsy is a matter of degree.

The relevance of all this for mystical experience is apparent. If physical disturbances in the brain can produce elaborate hallucinations that on occasion are, for the patient, indistinguishable from reality, may not such disturbances be the cause of all the experiences described as mystical? Is there, in short, any way of establishing that 'genuine' mystical experience ever occurs?

I do not think we can decide this question from our knowledge of physiology. Even if we had a full understanding of the brain state of, say, a God-conscious man, this would not enable us to tell whether his way of perceiving the world corresponded to reality. So far as physiological factors are concerned we are compelled to accept what Stace calls the principle of causal indifference. If an experience which would be judged mystical by all other criteria is found to arise from an 'unsatisfactory' cause—a migraine aura, for instance—it cannot be ruled out of consideration on that score alone. A case in point is that of Boehme, one of whose profoundest experiences was triggered by staring at a polished pewter vessel.[1]

At any given moment the quality of one's awareness depends on the state of one's nervous system. If, therefore, a migraine attack, a drug, or anything else produces the right physiological condition, a mystical experience will ensue. This is, in fact, the principle on which transcendental meditation is based. Maharishi is quite emphatic about this. 'The experience of the transcendental, impersonal God necessitates a particular condition of the nervous system. If this activity in the nervous system could be produced by physiological means, then this would be the physiological approach to realising the impersonal God.' (*SBAL*, p. 281.)

There is thus no difficulty in principle in understanding why patients with epilepsy or migraine may have experiences resembling those of the mystics. One has merely to assume that the pathological process gives rise to a state of the nervous system having some features in common with those that

---

[1] 'To plead the organic cause of a religious state of mind . . . in refutation of its claim to possess superior spiritual value, is quite illogical and arbitrary, unless one has already worked out in advance some psycho-physical theory connecting spiritual values in general with determinate sorts of physical change. Otherwise none of our thoughts and feelings, not even our *dis*beliefs, could retain any value as revelations of the truth, for every one of them without exception flows from the state of its possessor's body at the time.' (James, *VRE*, p. 36.)

determine the occurrence of mystical experience. About epilepsy our present ignorance is large, and about migraine it is larger, as Sacks makes plain; and of the neurophysiology of 'higher' states of consciousness we know almost nothing. But there seems no *a priori* reason why some similarities should not exist.

However, this is not at all to say that all mystical experience has a pathological cause. Because a man sees a hallucinatory crocodile, this does not mean that real crocodiles do not exist. Part of the difficulty, I think, arises from the vagueness of the term 'mysticism', which is used to embrace a great many phenomena some of which are certainly pathological.

My subject is not mysticism in general, however, but only that portion of it which is related to Maharishi's seven states of consciousness. All the higher states in this scheme come about through the practice of transcendental meditation; which, as I have tried to make clear, is in no sense a technique for producing abnormal physiological states; on the contrary, it consists in letting the body go in the direction it naturally wishes to take.

This point seems to me quite fundamental. Grey Walter remarks on the close dependence of brain metabolism on oxygen supply, and the way in which this supply can be reduced by certain manipulations of breathing. 'Such exercises in breath control and respiratory arrest are an essential part of many mystical practices, for example Yoga, and they undoubtedly contribute to the reported sensations as of abstraction, insight, and levitation.' (Op. cit., p. 17.) Now none of this has any place in transcendental meditation, in which breathing is not interfered with in any way and the amount of oxygen in the blood remains normal. (See Appendix.) Other techniques for inducing 'mystical' experience, such as sensory deprivation or the use of drugs, are likewise not relevant to transcendental meditation.

I conclude that the transcendental state is one into which the body sinks *naturally* in the right circumstances, and that—if one does choose to evaluate experiences on the basis of the 'normality' of their physiological substrate—the transcendental state has at least as good a claim to be a source of knowledge about reality as does the waking state. The same argument will apply to cosmic consciousness, God consciousness, and Unity, since these are based on the transcendental state.

This is to restrict oneself to physiology. But I think that we must agree with James that arguments from origins are unsatisfactory. 'Origin in immediate intuition; origin in pontifical authority; origin in supernatural revelation, as by vision, hearing, or unaccountable impression; origin in direct possession by a higher spirit, expressing itself in prophecy and warning; origin in automatic utterance generally—these have been stock warrants for the truth of one opinion after another which we find represented in religious history. The medical materialists are therefore only so many belated dogmatists, neatly turning the tables on their predecessors by using the criterion of origin in a destructive instead of an accreditive way.' (*VRE*, p. 40.)

For James, the pragmatist, the test of a belief is its results. But here a warning is necessary. Maharishi, as I have said before, insists that the insights of one state cannot be judged from the standpoint of a lower one. Suppose someone says he sees the world illuminated in the light of God. This is not so much a belief as a direct perception. Can we call it a hallucination? Certainly it does not resemble a dream or a vision. And it is apparently universally verifiable, at least in principle. It is, I think, more like a value judgement in aesthetics. One man finds the St Matthew Passion the greatest imaginable experience in music; another thinks it a bore. The differences, presumably, have a neurophysiological explanation; but how can one prove that one way of experiencing the sounds that make up the music is 'truer' than the other? Only by cultivating one's taste for music until one is able to appreciate Bach's quality; in other words, I suppose, by modifying one's nervous system to register the finer aesthetic aspects of music.

The same is true, I suggest, of perception of the world at large; the 'subtler' aspects are only perceptible to those who have undergone the necessary preparation.

In comparing at least some forms of mystical experience to aesthetic appreciation I am coming nearer to the alternative, psychological, approach which I mentioned at the beginning of this chapter; I mean the view that mysticism serves a psychological function. This is the subject which will occupy me in chapter X, but before coming to it I should like to look at some other attempts to approach mystical experience from a predominantly physicalist angle.

# CHAPTER IX

## *Enlightenment in Capsules*

AT THE PRESENT time a book like this cannot avoid mention of psychedelic drugs. What, if any, is the relation of the bizarre states which they may produce to Maharishi's seven states of consciousness?

I think the first point to establish is that drugs, though certainly most prominent in the public mind, are by no means the only, or even the most powerful, means of producing bizarre experiences. This comes out with great clarity in Charles T. Tart's anthology *Altered States of Consciousness* (Wiley, 1969), in which only two out of the seven sections are devoted to drugs. One of the most extraordinary studies of all—Tart's own experiment in 'mutual hypnosis' (ibid, pp. 291–308) has nothing to do with drugs.

In this experiment two subjects, under Tart's supervision, hypnotized each other. Not only did both subjects go into trances of much greater depth than they had achieved before; there was also a strong suggestion that they had been in tele-pathic communication with each other. The subjects them-selves believed this, and even came to feel that they had in some sense actually been 'in' the other-worldly places they seemed to have 'visited'. 'This was frightening to both [subjects], for what had seemed a lovely shared *fantasy* now threatened to be something *real*.' (Ibid., p. 306.) At times there was a feeling of merging with each other. 'This seemed like a partial fusion of identities, a partial loss of the distinction between Thou and I. This was felt to be good at the time, but later the [subjects] perceived this as a threat to their individual autonomy.' (Ibid., p. 306.)

What comes irresistibly to my mind when I read this paper is the description of the *Bardo* plane in the *Tibetan Book of the Dead*.

Hypnosis figures again in Milton H. Erickson's account (ibid., pp. 45–71) of some experiments which he carried out with the late Aldous Huxley. Huxley's experiments are, again, quite as remarkable as anything which people have reported after taking LSD.

Hypnosis is not the only means apart from drugs of producing altered states of consciousness. Another, which is within the experience of everyone, is dreaming. Here again the possibilities are a good deal wider than is generally realized. Dreams can be far more varied in quality as well as content than one would gather from the casebooks of most psycho-analysts. (On this, see van Eeden's classic paper 'A Study of Dreams', ibid., pp. 145–58.)

The point I wish to make is that drugs are simply one method, and possibly not the most effective one, of stimulating the brain to produce strange states of awareness. Hence in assessing the relevance of drugs to mystical experience in general and to the seven states of consciousness in particular, I return to Stace's principle of causal indifference; if a drug, or anything else, produces the right state in the brain, a mystical experience will ensue. The question at issue is thus not whether drugs *can* produce mystical experience, but whether they ever do.

A paper by Walter N. Pahnke and William A. Richards (ibid., pp. 399–428) suggests that psychedelic drugs can produce most of the phenomena of spontaneous mystical experience. The authors list nine inter-related categories of drug-induced mystical experience, which they derived from a survey of mystical literature and commentaries on such literatures, including the works of Stace and William James. The categories are as follows.

'1. Unity.'

This, the authors explain, can occur in either of two forms, internal or external. 'Internal unity occurs when consciousness merges with this "ground of being", beyond all empirical distinctions. Although awareness of one's own empirical ego has ceased, one does not become unconscious.' To illustrate this, the authors quote from a patient's description: 'I seemed to relinquish my life in "layers": the more I let go, the greater the sense of oneness I received. As I approached what I firmly believed to be the point of death, I experienced an ever greater sense of an eternal dimension to life.' (Ibid., p. 401.) The parallel with Tennyson's account (p. 49) is evident.

External unity, on the other hand, seems to occur when 'awareness of one or more particular sense impressions grows in intensity until suddenly the object of perception and the empirical ego simultaneously seem to cease to exist as separate entities, while consciousness seems to transcend subject and object and become impregnated by a profound sense of unity, accompanied by the insight that ultimately "all is One".

Stace accepts that the drug-induced experience may sometimes be indistinguishable from the natural extrovertive mystical experience, but he does not believe that it resembles the introvertive type. (*MP*, p. 30.) However, the descriptions I have just quoted suggest that drugs can produce at least a fair approximation to both types. Whether this is really so or not could only, I think, be pronounced on decisively by an expert— that is, by someone who was himself in the state of Unity. In any case, it seems probable that people might use very similar language to describe quite different experiences.

'2. Objectivity and Reality.'

This refers to James' 'noetic quality'. The insights gained are 'intuitively felt to be of a more fundamental form of reality than either the phenomena of everyday consciousness or the most vivid of dreams or hallucinations. A subject said: "I was experiencing directly the metaphysical theory known as emanationism in which, beginning with the clear, unbroken and infinite light of God, the light then breaks into forms and lessens in intensity as it passes through descending degrees of reality.... The emanation theory, and especially the elaborately worked-out layers of Hindu and Buddhist cosmology and psychology had heretofore been concepts and inferences. Now they were objects of the most direct and immediate perception. I could see exactly how these theories would have come into being if their progenitors had had this experience. But beyond accounting for their origin, my experience testified to their absolute truth." ' (Ibid., p. 403.)

'3. Transcendence of Space and Time.'
This again is commonly reported in mystical literature.

'4. Sense of Sacredness.'
'Inherent in the nondifferentiated unity of mystical consciousness is a profound sense of holiness and sacredness that is felt
to be at a more basic level than any religious or philosophical
concepts held by the experiencer.' (Ibid., pp. 403–4.) This is
significant. It relates to the qualities of the Absolute listed
earlier as grounds for identifying it with God (see p. 99).
Notice particularly that the sense of sacredness is quite
independent of the subject's previous beliefs.

'5. Deeply-Felt Positive Mood.'
This refers to feelings of joy, blessedness, and peace—'the
peace which passes understanding'. It is, in fact, the bliss-
quality of the Absolute.

'6. Paradoxicality.'
'This category reflects the manner in which significant aspects
of mystical experience are felt by the experiencer to be true in
spite of the fact that they violate the laws of Aristotelian logic . . .
[The subject] may envision a universal self that is both un-
qualitied and qualitied, both impersonal and personal, and both
inactive and active.' (Ibid., pp. 404–5.)
Paradoxicality is a very characteristic feature of mystical
experience. However, its occurrence in drug-induced states
does not prove that these are the same as spontaneous mystical
experience. In his book *The Use of Lateral Thinking* (Cape),
Edward de Bono has described how he caused a hypnotized subject to have the illusion of seeing a square circle, a violently
paradoxical experience, which the subject sought frantically to
convey. Here we have *one* feature of mystical awareness and—as
in the case of migraine auras—the differences are as important
as the resemblances.

'7. Alleged Ineffability.'
The authors suggest that the cause of this is the inadequacy
of language, which in turn arises out of the paradoxicality and
uniqueness of the experience.

'8. Transiency.'

Drug-induced mystical states last for between a few seconds and a few hours. This transiency, according to the authors, is an important point of difference between such states and psychosis. I shall return to this later.

'9. Positive Changes in Attitude and/or Behaviour.'

People who have drug-induced experiences claim improvements in their attitudes towards themselves, others, and life in general; they also report increased self-integration. How real these changes may be is still uncertain.

'Mystical' experiences are, of course, by no means the rule when psychedelic drugs are taken. Many factors, including personality, circumstances, and expectations, seem to influence the outcome. However, the possibility that a 'mystical' experience will result and the belief that the benefits claimed for such experiences, even when drug-induced, are real has led a number of psychiatrists, especially in the United States and Canada, to use psychedelic drugs as a short cut to self-integration. Similar reasoning seems to underlie at least some of the interest in these drugs shown by people who take them illegally.

Many psychiatrists have denied that the drug experience does really improve self-integration at all. I have quoted the opinion of Pahnke and Richards in some detail because I wanted to put the case for the therapeutic value of psychedelic drugs as fairly as possible, but I certainly do not wish to endorse the claims which have been made on behalf of these drugs. I feel that the question is still quite open. What I wish to do is to show how the theoretical basis for these claims relates to the theoretical basis of transcendental meditation. In other words, are drugs and meditation different ways of trying to achieve the same end?

In the first place, I think we have to admit that, since the fundamental changes brought about by transcendental meditation are neurophysiological, they could conceivably be duplicated by a drug. However, this must remain for the foreseeable future a theoretical possibility only, for the reason that transcendental meditation seems to affect the nervous system and body as a whole, whereas drugs produce more or less localized effects on target organs. The hallucinogenic drugs, for example, seem to have a disruptive effect on interneuronal communications within the brain by competing with the natural neurotransmitters for their receptor sites. (See J. R. Smythies, 'Schizophrenia and the Mechanism of Action of Hallucinogenic Drugs', *Abstracts of World Medicine*, vol. 44, 1970, pp. 489–97.) The difference seems to be that drugs produce their effects by distorting the normal action of the brain, whereas transcendental meditation merely allows a different physiological state to occur. To reproduce all the effects of transcendental meditation one would have to have a complete understanding of physiology; and this, if it can ever be achieved at all, is almost infinitely remote. There is no drug used today that does not have some unwanted effects and, in general, the more powerful the drug the more dangerous its unwanted effects. This is certainly true of the hallucinogens.

Secondly, there is a basic difference between drugs and transcendental meditation in the way they are used. Clinically, psychedelic drugs are used in two ways: either they are given periodically, in small doses, as an adjunct to ordinary methods of psychotherapy, or else they are given in a single large dose to induce rapid and profound changes in the way the person thinks about himself and the world. It is the second method which can produce mystical experiences. Its success apparently depends on the profundity of experience; but unpleasant, 'nadir' experiences are, it seems, as valuable as pleasant, 'peak' ones. (See the paper by Robert E. Mogar in *Altered States of Consciousness*, pp. 393–7.)

The principle of this form of therapy is thus to try to produce, within a short space of time, what might be called a 'personality earthquake', with consequent release of tension and reorientation of the lines of force within the personality. It is easy to understand that this can, on occasion, be distressing.

I think the sort of mechanism I am considering has an interesting bearing on certain types of natural mystical experience. It is well known that a number of great mystics were subject to frequent ill-health, and, as we saw in Chapter VII, this has sometimes been used as a means of discrediting their pronouncements. I concluded that, in so doing, medical materialism went too far. But what is the reason for the association between mysticism and ill-health?[1] Evelyn Underhill attributes it to the inability of the body to sustain the intensity of mystical transports: 'Our bodies are animal things, made for animal activities. When a spirit of unusual ardour insists on using its nerve-cells for other activities, they kick against the pricks; and inflict, as the mystics themselves acknowledge, the penalty of "mystical ill-health".' (*Mysticism*, Methuen, 1904, p. 61.)

Marghanita Laski also remarks on the association of mysticism with suffering, though she does not attempt to account for it. She illustrates it with quotations from Emily Brontë:

Oh, dreadful is the check—intense the agony
When the ear begins to hear and the eye begins to see;
When the pulse begins to throb, the brain to think again,
The soul to feel the flesh and the flesh to feel the chain!

Yet I would lose no sting, would wish no torture less;
The more that anguish racks the earlier it will bless;
And robed in fires of Hell, or bright with heavenly shine,
If it but herald Death, the vision is divine.
(From *The Prisoner*),

and from Suso:

This ecstasy lasted from half an hour to an hour, and whether his soul were in the body or out of the body he could not tell. But when he came to his senses it seemed to him that he returned from another world. And so greatly did his body suffer in this short rapture that it seemed to him that none, even in dying, could suffer so greatly in so short a time. The

---

[1] This association is by no means the rule, and indeed mystical experience normally has the reverse effect, actually enhancing physical health. Mystics tend to be long-lived. Transcendental meditation, likewise, appears to improve physical as well as mental well-being. (See Appendix.)

Servitor [sc. Suso] came to himself moaning, and he fell down upon the ground like a man who swoons. And he cried inwardly, heaving great sighs from the depth of his soul and saying, 'Oh, my God, where was I and where am I?' And again, 'Oh, my heart's joy, never shall my soul forget this hour!' (E. Underhill, *Mysticism*, pp. 187–8.)

Notice that although both authors compare their pains to what they imagine death must be like, neither fails to welcome them as the necessary concomitant of the most intense joy.

I would tentatively interpret the painful aspect of these experiences as arising from the sudden and uncontrolled release of great tension. In the case of the natural mystics such release occurs when the pressure becomes too great. The effect of drugs seems to be to release it before it reaches such intensity. An important feature of drug-induced 'mysticism' that has been noted both by psychologists and by drug-takers themselves is that the drugs do not appear to produce the experiences but only to release them in people who are ripe for them. In general, drug-takers get the kind of experience they deserve. However, there seems to be a tendency for 'bad trips' to succeed good ones, and this suggests—what seems probable on other grounds—that repeated use of these extraordinarily powerful substances may produce neurological damage.

The regular practice of transcendental meditation seems to allow tensions to be released *gradually*. In this respect it could be compared to the methods which have been proposed for preventing earthquakes by pumping water as a lubricant into the faults in the earth's crust when movement is occurring; the movement still occurs, but in a controlled fashion.

From the practical point of view, this means that transcendental meditation should not be judged by whether it produces dramatic experiences. It may do so at times; but it does not depend on these for success. A gradual accumulation of small changes is as good, in some ways better than, one large one. The goal of meditation is not to produce strange experiences, however interesting these may be, but only to achieve and make permanent the state of self-awareness and then to develop this to Unity.

To concentrate on psychological experiences is misleading in another way also. Transcendental meditation is, as I have said, concerned purely with removing the physiological effects of stress. It is therefore not necessary to try to understand or 'assimilate' experiences. This saves a great deal of confusion. Interpretations can always be disputed, but transcendental meditation goes beyond the level of interpretation. To me this seems a mark of Maharishi's originality; in one sense he out- does the medical materialists, for he fully admits the impor- tance of the physical basis of psychology; and yet he does not sacrifice spirituality.

The proof of the pudding is, of course, the eating. Is transcendental meditation more effective than drugs in 'restructuring' the personality? For formal evidence that it is we shall have to await the outcome of studies already being undertaken and planned. But already there are signs. One of the most encouraging is the tendency for people who have been taking drugs—of all kinds—to reduce their use and, usually, give them up when they start practising transcendental meditation. The usual pattern seems to be for the drugs to lose their attraction and even their effectiveness. If this trend is finally confirmed by objective research its importance in the present time will not have to be spelled out.

The gradual but progressive nature of transcendental meditation has its counterpart in the permanency of the effects it produces. Here we come to a point of great importance, which I have already touched on. Some psychologists who favour the use of psychedelic drugs make brevity of duration an essential characteristic of mystical experience—one which helps to differentiate it from psychosis. This would make the states I have called God consciousness and Unity into psychoses; a conclusion which I clearly cannot accept. So where does the difference lie?

I think at least part of the difference between Maharishi's higher states of consciousness and the psychoses is the same as that which exists between the 'natural' brief mystical ex- perience and the results of pathological processes such as migraine: namely, the 'wholeness' of the normal experience. The form of psychosis which approaches nearest to God consciousness is, I suppose, mania, but even here there are many differences. Objectively, mania, if at all severe, is perceptible to other people; the patient is voluble, excited and so on. God consciousness, on the other hand, is, as Maharishi insists, not marked by any special form of behaviour. This is a point evidently not appreciated by Zaehner, who, basing his position on the case of John Custance,[1] thinks that the difference between mania and 'nature mysticism' (by which he seems to mean all forms of extrovertive mystical experience which do not lead the mystic to speak of a personal God) is only one of degree. 'The loosening of the moral sense, or . . . its diversion from its normal channels, is, of course, what is most liable to bring the maniac into conflict with the authorities, or, as in Mr. Custance's case, with his own material interests and those of his family. Thus, when a man sees in every street-walker a consecrated hierodule and, out of reverence almost, gives her hundreds of pounds, there is every chance of trouble.' (*Mysticism Sacred and Profane*, p. 89.)

Subjectively, too, there are important differences. I suspect the position is confused by a measure of uncertainty about terminology. Zaehner, for example, says: 'it cannot be denied that the manic and the natural mystical experience leave with all those who have had it an overwhelming sense that what they have experienced is not only real in a sense that ordinary sense experience is not, but also that it has a profound meaning.' (Op. cit., p. 96.) On the other hand Miss Laski takes a different view '. . . ecstatics usually are and remain convinced of the value of any beliefs they may derive from their experiences; beliefs derived when in states accepted as those of mental disease are not usually regarded as valuable once the patient is cured.' (*Ecstasy*, p. 257.)

There seems to be a contradiction here. Is the explanation perhaps that mania comprises more than one kind of disorder? And may *some* sorts of mania afford glimpses into reality? If so, one could suppose that the behaviour of the manic patient is abnormal, not because he has seen too far into reality, but because he has not seen far enough.

[1] John Custance is a sufferer from manic-depression who has written of his experiences in two books.

God consciousness, because it has evolved on the basis of permanent Self-awareness in cosmic consciousness, is a fully integrated state, in which the mind can operate on many levels simultaneously. Mania, on the other hand, is a condition of excitement and confusion.

Certainly all descriptions of mania seem poles away from the deep tranquillity which, to my ear at least, comes so convincingly across the gulf of time and thought that separates us from St Catherine of Genoa:

When the loving kindness of God calls a soul from the world, He finds it full of vices and sins; and at first he gives it an instinct for virtue, and then urges it to perfection, and then by infused grace leads it to true self-naughting, and at last to true transformation. And this noteworthy order serves God to lead the soul along the Way; but when the soul is naughted and transformed, then of herself she neither works nor speaks nor wills, nor feels nor hears nor understands, neither has she of herself the feeling of outward or inward, where she may move. And in all things it is God who rules and guides her, without the mediation of any creature. And the state of this soul is then a feeling of such utter peace and tranquillity that it seems to her that her heart, and her bodily being, and all both within and without is immersed in an ocean of utmost peace; from whence she shall never come forth for anything that can befall her in this life. And she stays immovable, imperturbable, impassible. So much so, that it seems to her in her human and spiritual nature, both within and without, she can feel no other thing than sweetest peace. And she is so full of peace that though she press her flesh, her nerves, her bones, no other thing comes forth from them than peace. Then says she all day for joy such rhymes as these, making them according to her manner:

> Vuoi tu che tu mostr'io
> Presto che cosa e Dio?
> Pace non trova chi da lui si partio.[1]

(Quoted in Evelyn Underhill, *Mysticism*, p. 440.)

[1] Shall I tell you what God is? Away from him no one can find peace.—*A.C.*

# CHAPTER X

## *Creativity*

THERE ARE, AS we saw on pp. 112–13, two main modern approaches to the study of mysticism. One is to say that *all* mystical experience is pathological; I have already given reasons why I think this view should be rejected. Another approach, which implicitly underlay many of the passages which I quoted in Chapter IX, seems to be becoming increasingly popular among 'progressive' psychologists; it might perhaps be described as non-committal benevolence. Its underlying assumption (which is seldom made explicit) is that one can explain (not explain away) mysticism in purely psychological terms, without reference to an Absolute.

Let me make clear what this would imply. It would imply that mystical experience has a function, which could perhaps be called the promotion of self-integration, but that its claims to provide direct awareness of the nature of reality are at best dubious and at worst invalid. (I have already touched on this problem with reference to the state of pure awareness in Chapter VI, but I should like to return to it here and treat it in a rather wider context.)

On this question most psychologists sympathetic to mysticism, such as Maslow, preserve a discreet silence. Non-professionals like myself, not having a position to keep up, can afford to be more explicit.

One non-professional whose views seem to me of the greatest interest is Marghanita Laski. In her remarkable study *Ecstasy*, to which I have already referred, she advances a sympathetic but openly atheistic view of mysticism. She decisively rejects the view that all mystical experience can be ascribed to pathology. 'While some pathological states can undoubtedly produce experiences in some or many ways similar to what I have called intensity ecstasies [see p. 106], it seems to me certain that these experiences are typically produced in people of good mental and physical health.' (*Ecstasy*, p. 254.) Equally, however, she rejects the 'spiritual', and instead puts forward a subtle and original argument which I can do no more than call attention to, but which cannot be ignored in any discussion of these experiences.

Her theory is, in brief, that intensity ecstasy is linked to the synthesis of mental material. It is, in fact, an accompaniment of the rearrangement of ideas which we call creativity. Ecstatic experience is valued, Miss Laski believes, not primarily for the delight it brings—which is great—but because of its association with the organizing, creative power of the mind. Its occurrence is thus a sign of psychological good health.

'I do not believe,' Miss Laski writes, 'that any explanations of these experiences can be satisfactory if they suggest that ecstasies are *only* this or *only* that—only a phenomenon of repressed sexuality or only a concomitant of some or other morbid condition. Certainly convictions are an insufficient substitute for evidence, but both people's convictions of the value of these experiences and their subsequent influence on outlook and language persuade me that these are of some evidential value in justifying the conclusion that ecstatic experiences must be treated as important outside religious contexts, as having important effects on people's mental and physical well-being, on their aesthetic preferences, their creativity, their beliefs and philosophies, and on their conduct.' (*Ecstasy*, p. 373.)

Miss Laski's theory is the most successful attempt so far, I think, to explain mysticism on a purely psychological basis. Whether such attempts can ever be wholly successful is another question, which I shall discuss a little later.

It is an essential part of her theory that creativity does not depend on the literal 'inspiration' of anything that was not originally in the mind, but consists wholly in the rearrangement of existing ideas. (I suppose one could compare the creative act to shaking a kaleidoscope, and the ecstatic experience which may accompany it to the sensation of pleasure that the viewer obtains from the new pattern.)

I myself find her ideas stimulating. In particular, her theory has the merit of providing common ground for conversion, inspiration, and response to art. I am sure she is right in holding that although these experiences differ from one another in degree of intensity they are not unrelated; they could be arranged along a spectrum. Even the trivial cannot be excluded: 'in all trivial creative products, we still have examples of new form. Either we must say that exalted ideas and purposes probably spring from one kind of process and trivial ideas and purposes from another, or we must accept the probability that similar processes lie behind all inspirations, no matter what their scale or value.' (*Ecstasy*, p. 287.)

This last point seems to me particularly important; yet I feel that Miss Laski fails to bring out its full significance, for the interesting reason that her implied model of the mind is too simple. While I basically agree that creativity can be explained in terms of psychological dynamics, for the reasons I have discussed earlier I do not think these dynamics can be accommodated except in a 'depth' model such as is hinted at by the tripartite structure I have put forward.

If we adopt a model of this kind we can certainly allow for Miss Laski's main conclusions, especially her unified concept of creativity that links the trivial to the sublime. Thus, for Maharishi, *every* thought springs from the deepest layers of the mind, but is only appreciated consciously when it reaches the superficial level of ordinary awareness. Reorganization of mental material goes on in the depths, at the subtle levels. Creativity consists in the ability to appreciate and make use of these subtle levels, and this ability in turn depends on the capacity of the individual *to allow his mind to become still*. One cannot see into the depths of a pool unless the surface is perfectly calm.

On this basis one can, I think, understand why many people report that transcendental meditation enhances creativity.[1] The creative process consists typically in an alternation between repose and activity. In whatever field the creativity expresses itself, this seems to be true. Here, for example, is that most perspicacious of counsellors, the late F. L. Lucas, advising on methods of writing:

[1] 'The extensive work on creativity by MacKinnon and his associates indicates that the truly creative person is distinguished from the noncreative by his capacity for "transliminal experience". Following Harold Rugg's study of creative imagination, the transliminal experience is characterized by an illuminating flash of insight occurring at a critical threshold of the conscious-unconscious continuum.' (Robert E. Mogar, in *Altered States of Consciousness*, p. 397.)

'A great part of the writer's problem . . . is how to catch the ideas that creep forth in the *stillness* [my italics], like magic mice, from their holes. Here I suspect that the dog's method is less effective than the cat's. "Wise passiveness" may succeed better than impatient rush and pounce. No doubt the artist or the thinker may carry his day-dreaming to excess, so that it becomes a vice—Balzac called it "smoking enchanted cigars". But it pays, I think, to meditate[1] a good deal, both before beginning to write, and at intervals while writing. The processes of creation may refuse to be bustled.' (*Style*, Pan edition, 1964, p. 226.)

Maharishi emphasizes the same point:

'The strokes of the artist's brush gain their certainty and vitality through the depth of his moments of silence interspersing his painting activity. . . . While he is creating, every little moment of rest brings the enlivening of awareness so that the next stroke is more creative. . . . The number and depth of those moments in the production of a work directly influence the true value of the product. Bringing our consciousness repeatedly to pure creativity and intelligence eventually brings pure creativity and intelligence into all our conscious life.' (*Creative Intelligence*, 1971, No. 1, p. 3.)

The growth of creativity through the practice of transcendental meditation is progressive. At first, access to the deepest layers is attained only during meditation. But with repeated experience of transcending the ability to reach these deeper layers grows, and ultimately, in cosmic consciousness, it becomes complete and permanent. Then *every* action is based upon the stillness of the Absolute.

Such a view of creativity agrees with the account of scientific method advanced by, among others, Karl Popper. On this hypothesis, science proceeds, not by Baconian induction (amassing large numbers of facts until eventually a theory emerges through generalization), but by a sort of imaginative pattern-weaving. This brings scientific activity nearer to art; for although naturally the theories, once propounded, must be tested by

[1] Not meditation in the sense I am using the word, of course. But Lucas' choice of the word is none the less a happy one.

experiment to see whether they match the facts, the creative heart of the process lies in the dreaming.

'Let us learn to dream gentlemen. Then, perhaps, we shall find the truth . . . but let us beware of publishing our dreams before they have been put to the proof by the waking understanding.'[1] (A. Kekulé, quoted James H. Leuba, *Principles of Religious Mysticism*, London, p. 242n.)

Kekulé himself provides one of the best examples of the effectiveness of this sort of 'dreaming', in his account of how he discovered the benzene ring structure—one of the fundamental building blocks in organic chemistry. He had been working on a chemistry textbook, but without much success:

'. . . My spirit was with other things. I turned my chair to the fireplace and sank into a half-sleep. Again the atoms flitted before my eyes. . . . Long rows, variously, more closely united; all in movement, wriggling and turning like snakes. And see, what was that? One of the snakes seized its own tail and the image whirled scornfully before my eyes. As though from a flash of lightning I awoke; this time again I occupied the rest of the night in working out the consequences of the hypothesis.' (Quoted in Stanley Burnshaw, *The Seamless Web*, Penguin, p. 177.)

This is a fascinating passage. Kekulé had clearly gone into a 'subtle' state of awareness, which he calls half-sleep. (Note that, like Bucke in the passage I quoted on pp. 99–100, he was not

---

[1] Inspiration—access to the deeper layers—is not enough by itself; there must be 'surface' knowledge and skill as well. Someone who has never tried to write a poem before is unlikely to produce a good one in response to inspiration, however great; the world may well be full of mute inglorious Miltons. (Indeed, there is some evidence that previous intellectual work at the 'surface' level is an important factor facilitating the subsequent inspiration.) The new theory, the draft for the poem, the idea for the novel, must be assessed intellectually and at this stage may be modified or rejected outright. Lack of the necessary intellectual or practical groundwork is probably one reason for the badness of some new ideas. Another, I think, is that few people, even the most creative, have *regular* access to deeper layers of awareness. Spontaneous ecstasy is typically rare, and may be experienced but once in a lifetime. It can hardly be possible to take in all the details of a whole new world at a single glance, and hence the insights obtained 'at depth' may arrive at the surface in a distorted condition, like deep-sea fish that burst open when brought up to the surface.

For someone who has developed the ability to operate on all levels systematically, however, the position is different. Inspiration is then not a sudden uprush but a controlled flow. This has obvious advantages. A gushing oil well is certainly dramatic; but it is also wasteful and, if it goes on fire, possibly dangerous.

trying to direct his thoughts; he simply 'slipped'.) At this level his problem solved itself.

I think we may conclude from this discussion that Miss Laski is right in her contention that creativity of every kind is all of a piece, and that therefore one cannot draw absolute distinctions between science and art or between important inspirations and trivial ones. I think she is also right in regarding ecstasy as closely related to creativity. However, her determination to explain ecstatic experience in *wholly* psychological terms leads her, I feel, to an untenable position. I will try to illustrate this by some specific examples.

Miss Laski, like many other writers on mysticism, recognizes the existence of two types of mysticism, which she calls respectively 'intensity' and 'withdrawal'. (I have already discussed this on p. 106, and I pointed out there that her 'withdrawal' type, which she associates particularly with Eastern mysticism, is similar to Stace's introvertive experience—in fact, it is transcending.) She realizes that 'withdrawal' and 'intensity' experiences are somehow related, and indeed she says: 'I think it probable that all intensity experiences begin by being, to no matter how slight a degree, withdrawal ones.' (Op. cit., p. 369.) On Maharishi's theory, of course, this is just what one would expect; the preliminary 'withdrawal' is the 'dive', which results in the subsequent 'intensity' experience. (There are many suggestions of physical changes, especially affecting the breathing, during intensity ecstasy. This again is what one would expect.)

Another problem is the duration of ecstasy. Miss Laski, like William James, believes that ecstasy is typically brief, and indeed she comes close to making brevity a criterion of ecstasy. However, she does recognize the existence of 'unitive states'—prolonged, even permanent, ecstatic states. 'To attain such a condition is the aim of most people who have assumed a supernatural origin for ecstasies. Such a condition, when habitual, must clearly involve some . . . transformation of the "higher faculties" . . ., and it seems probable that the way to it must be one of such unremitting and systematized mental discipline as all [*sic*] mystical religions and philosophies have evolved for those who seek it.' (*Ecstasy*, pp. 63–64.)

These prolonged ecstatic states are obviously hard to accommodate in her theory; it is difficult to see how reorganization of mental material could continue indefinitely. For Maharishi, however, the permanent duration of higher states of consciousness is the norm; it is the inability to maintain them which is abnormal. This inability arises when the nervous system has not been progressively adapted (by regular coming to transcendental consciousness) to sustain them.

Here, then, are two (on Miss Laski's theory) puzzling features of ecstatic experience which fall into place in Maharishi's scheme of seven states of consciousness.

There is, however, a more general objection, not only to Miss Laski's theory, but to any theory of mysticism which accepts the experiences as immensely, even supremely, valuable to the individual but denies them more than a purely subjective validity. All such theories, I think, wish to have things both ways. For if one accepts that a mystical experience can be the most important event in a person's life yet persists in rejecting the notion of an Absolute to which such experiences usually give rise, one finds oneself in the curious position of maintaining that the more complete the experience (the closer it comes to the state of Unity) the profounder the error into which it plunges the unfortunate ecstatic. It is surely difficult to accept that an experience can be at once supremely valuable and totally deceptive. For my part at least I find it easier to believe, with Broad (see note on p. 112), that mystical experience does indeed bring man into contact with transcendental Reality.

To see mystical experience in this wide—indeed, universal—context is, I believe, to see it truly. And if creativity and mystical experience are indeed intimately intertwined, creativity too ought to be looked at in a wide context. This has been done by the biologist E. W. Sinnott. The creative process in man, he says, depends on the existence in the 'unconscious' of an organizing factor, which selects ideas and fits them into new patterns. What is this organizing factor? It is, Sinnott suggests, life itself.

'What, then, may we conclude as to the biological basis of creativity? Simply this, I think: that *life* itself is the creative process by virtue of its organizing, pattern-forming, questing quality, its most distinctive character. In living things below man and in man's bodily structure, life is tied to a conservative and relatively rigid physical basis in the genetic constitution of the individual, necessary if the world of organisms is not to become mixed and chaotic. But when this same organizing quality is applied to behaviour, its products are much more various; and when it operates in the unthinkable complexity of the human brain, with its billions of neurones and almost countless number of synapses, the possibilities of new mental patterns are almost infinite. . . . Here is the field where the creative imagination operates, whether in the conscious or unconscious mind. Imagination, we may say, is simply the basic formative quality of life, emerging at this highest level from its former dependence on a rigid material basis and free to express itself in high creativity. The material for these expressions, these new norms and patterns, may exist in many forms—in pigments on canvas, in musical notes, in words, or simply in ideas. However creativity may manifest itself in the affairs of men, it is in this inherent creativity of life, I believe, that its ultimate source is to be found.' (From *Creativity*, ed. P. E. Vernon, Penguin, pp. 113–14.)

The passage I have just quoted is so remarkably in tune with Maharishi's thinking that it might almost have been written by him. The creativity of life of which Sinnott speaks is referred to by Maharishi as 'creative intelligence'. 'Everywhere everything has its origin in one absolute existence. A man's creative intelligence has its origin in that one absolute existence, and so everything may be cognized in its maximum creative potentiality because absolute existence is absolutely creative. . . . We can say, too, that all relative expressions of creativity have their source in pure intelligence, since creative *intelligence* is both absolute and relative. The whole of individual and cosmic life is fundamentally creative because it goes on and on; it is progressive, evolutionary; and the whole of life is fundamentally intelligent because it proceeds systematically, containing its own order and unfolding in an overall orderly way, unifying individual purposes in a multipurpose flow.'[1] (Maharishi Mahesh Yogi, *Creative Intelligence*, 1971, No. 1, p. 2.)

[1] For some people these ideas may raise a difficulty. They suggest that creativity is essentially a joyful experience that comes to stress-free minds; yet it is quite

As Sinnott recognizes, suggestions of this kind are likely to be looked on askance by some. 'Many biologists will look with disfavour on an extrapolation of the fact of organization, real though it is, into the realm of purpose and thus of mind, and they will be likely to regard as useless the attempt to see in it the germ of creativity. Psychologists, particularly of the tougher-minded sort, will criticize the argument as naive and as offering to our understanding of creativeness little that is constructive. I cannot help feeling, however, that the roots of the various problems that have been discussed here will finally be found in an understanding of the nature of life. Biologists, like all good and conservative

---

common today to hear remarks such as 'I need my tensions if I am to be creative', or 'art comes from suffering'. And the case of artists like Van Gogh is often adduced in proof of the contention that suffering is a necessary precondition of artistic creation.

There is a quarter-truth lurking somewhere in these arguments, I think, but not much more. Yet even if the theory of art as based on suffering were right, it would not prove that suffering is in any sense a 'good thing'. Perhaps Van Gogh would not have painted so well if he had not suffered so much—or perhaps he would have painted better, we cannot know—but even if he had not painted at all, what then? The world would have been the poorer, no doubt, but what about Van Gogh?

The notion that suffering is the mainspring of art seems to have begun with the Romantics. It received semi-scientific endorsement from Freud; nevertheless it is, I think, largely a fallacy. Depth of feeling is not in itself a guarantee of artistic excellence—if anything, rather the reverse. For Wordsworth, poetry takes its origin from emotion recollected in *tranquillity*. Here is the crux of the matter: certainly the artist needs some spur to begin work, but the quality of that work depends on the silence from which it springs.

Artistic activity undoubtedly does release tension. But it does not follow that the greater the tension the finer the art; many people suffer the most appalling tension yet produce no art at all. It seems likely that there are two forms of artistic activity, which are not entirely distinct but represent opposite ends of a scale; at one end the role of tension is greatest, at the other it is least. Probably these differences are related to psychological and physiological differences in the artists concerned; one type of person may require a great deal of tension before he can create, while another requires very little. Van Gogh and Strindberg might serve as examples of the first group, Mozart and Bach of the second. I would expect that transcendental meditation would reduce the artistic activity of the first group, at least temporarily, and enhance that of the second. And so far as I can tell this expectation is borne out by the experience of meditators.

Our society sets a great deal of store by creativity; perhaps too much. The modern preoccupation with expressing oneself sometimes seems like a neurosis, a frenzied search for identity in a vast impersonal world where the individual counts for nothing. We tend to forget that a truly creative person will express his or her personality continuously and without trying. Nor is so-called 'art' the only form of creativity; a happy marriage, for example, or even a well-decorated room, may be a far more genuine creation than many a formal 'work of art'.

scientists, have hesitated to plunge into speculations which verge on the metaphysical, for both speculation and metaphysics are somewhat in disrepute in scientific circles today. But problems such as this one of creativeness are so involved with life that students of the science of life, whether they like it or not, are going to be impelled more and more to try to make some contribution towards their solution, if only to state the problems in a more precise form.' (Op. cit., pp. 114–15.)

Of course, not all scientists have been afraid to acknowledge the relationship between scientific inspiration and mysticism, and among those who have spoken out have been some of the very greatest. Here, for example, is Einstein:

'The most beautiful emotion we can experience is the mystical. It is the sower of all true art and science. He to whom this emotion is a stranger . . . is as good as dead. To know that what is impenetrable to us really exists, manifesting itself as the highest wisdom and the most radiant beauty, which our dull faculties can comprehend only in their most primitive forms—this knowledge, this feeling, is at the heart of true religiousness. In this sense, and in this sense only, I belong to the ranks of devoutly religious men.' (Quoted by Philipp Frank, *Einstein, His Life and Times*, pp. 340–1.)

Frank adds the following gloss: 'According to Einstein's conception, it is particularly the scientist in the field of natural science, and especially in the field of mathematical physics, who has this mystical experience.'

This last observation raises a most interesting idea. Physicists, more than biologists, are inclined to see connections between science and religion. Why? May it be because their branch of science is so much further advanced? Physics, working at the sub-atomic level, is close to the Absolute; it is operating in a region which is permeated, as it were, with the quality of the Absolute. No other branch of science, except perhaps astronomy, is in this region. ('The Absolute is smaller than the smallest, greater than the greatest.') I suspect it is no accident that it is the physicists and the astronomers (Einstein, Eddington, Jeans, Schrödinger) who come first to mind when one thinks of scientists who have speculated most boldly about the ultimate questions.

# CHAPTER XI

## *Desire*

THROUGHOUT THE LAST few chapters I have been looking at mysticism from a number of angles, and it seems to me that one general conclusion has emerged. While every approach I have examined—even the relatively simple-minded one of medical materialism—contained some measure of truth, none was ultimately satisfactory that did not allow the validity of the mystics' claim that their experience brought them into contact with transcendent Reality. The name given to this Reality—the Absolute, Brahman, Nirvana, God, Allah—is not of great importance, and inevitably reflects the background of the particular mystic. What seems to me most significant, however, is that even people without formal religious beliefs who have apparently 'secular' experiences induced by drugs, find themselves adopting, almost against their will, language that expresses a sense of the holy and sacred.

For these reasons I would say, quite uncompromisingly, that it is to the religious literature we must turn if we want the best understanding of mysticism. I do not mean that the religious literature should be accepted at its face value. What I would maintain, however, is that no writer who rejects the possibility of a transcendent Reality—or even who is too carefully non-committal about it—can give a balanced picture of mysticism.

The weaknesses of modern rationalist attitudes to religious mysticism are well exemplified in the article by Pahnke and Richards from which I have already quoted.

'Perhaps one of the reasons mysticism has come to be considered other-worldly in the sense of being an escape from social responsibilities lies not in the nature of mystical consciousness itself, but rather in the poor methods that have been used by men to gain such experience. The mediaeval monk in his darkened cell and the hermit in the deep recesses of his cave, for example, used not psychedelic substances, but the tools of sensory deprivation, sleep deprivation, meditative disciplines, and fasting to elicit biochemical changes and unlock the door to unconscious levels of mind. . . . It would appear logical to suggest that whenever altered forms of consciousness occur, whether they are anticipated or come as a complete surprise, underlying biochemical activity may be involved. Thus the Hindu yogin practising breath control or the Christian monk spending long hours in solitary prayer may be seen to be influencing body chemistry in the same direction as the modern man who ingests a psychedelic drug. In all seriousness, one may ask if the yogin or the monk has much time for social action when perhaps a major portion of his life is spent in withdrawal from the world. Furthermore, such ascetic practices are poor means of unlocking the unconscious and may be similar to the ingestion of extremely small doses of the psychedelics. . . . There is reason to think that other-worldliness may be a result, not of going too deep into the unconscious mind, but rather of not going deep enough. It seems significant that persons who have experienced mystical consciousness generally feel thrown back into the very heart of life in this world and feel also that they have been given the inner strength to cope with suffering and struggle in society. It would seem better for a person to have a drug-facilitated experience of mystical consciousness, enjoy the enriched life that may follow, and serve other persons during the greater part of his life than to live a life that may be inauthentic and withdrawn until old age, when such an experience may occur by means of ascetic practices.' (Op. cit., pp. 417–18.)

With one aspect of these authors' view I cannot quarrel. It is quite true that the recluse life is not the only—or even, for most people, the best—way of achieving full development. Maharishi is emphatic that the main reason for the backwardness of modern India and for the disrepute into which 'meditative' practices have fallen in the West is precisely confusion between the way of life of the recluse and that of the person living in the world. Similarly, according to Abbot Cuthbert Butler, during the early centuries of the Christian era 'contemplation' was not thought of as an exclusively recluse occupation but was enjoined upon all Christians. (See his *Western Mysticism*, passim, second edition, London, 1926.)

To this extent, then, Pahnke and Richards are in the right. However, to dismiss the whole history of religious mysticism in East and West as nothing but the record of attempts to produce psychedelic experiences by inadequate and outdated methods seems to me incredibly superficial.[1]

One important reason why I feel this is that Pahnke and Richards, like almost all writers who hold a brief for the psychedelic drugs, speak as if the aim of the great mystics of the past had been to produce 'experiences'. But, as I tried to bring out in the last chapter, the great mystics of the past were concerned, not merely with reaching the divine in flashes, but in becoming united with it permanently. They climbed to reach, not a peak, but a plateau. And, as I have tried to show, this is Maharishi's teaching also. Without further apology, therefore, I shall take up the rest of this chapter with an examination of some aspects of specifically religious mysticism.

I think it is true to say that the dominant note of almost all mysticism, Eastern and Western, is the need for freedom from the 'chains of the flesh'. Not only during meditation, but at other times also, the would-be mystic is exhorted to be without this or that—love of possessions, love of comfort, love of all that binds him to the world. Indeed, St John of the Cross goes further: not only secular attachments, but spiritual ones also, bind the soul. 'Self-denial has to be like a total temporal and spiritual death.' (*Ascent of Mount Carmel*, Book II, Chapter 7.)

The reasoning behind this idea is simple enough. The Absolute, the Godhead, is, so the argument runs, the supreme good of life; it is our common experience that we get nothing for nothing; therefore to gain the Absolute we must be prepared to sacrifice everything. One cannot have one's cake and eat it.

This argument rests on an even more fundamental assumption: that Absolute and relative, spiritual and material, are mutually incompatible. Such a belief inevitably suggests that the Absolute is to be gained by rejecting the material world. The material world being the field of individuality, to reject it means

[1] Note that the Krishna of the Bhagavad Gita specifically advises against the kind of austerities which Pahnke and Richards suppose to be the standard means of attaining mystical experience. 'Yoga, indeed, is not for him who eats too much nor for him who does not eat at all, O Arjuna; it is not for him who is too much given to sleep nor yet for him who keeps awake.' (*BG*, VI, 16.)

to nullify as far as possible the ordinary unregenerate self, with its pettinesses, meannesses, and trivial desires. There is moreover good authority for such an undertaking, for—in India particularly but also in the West—people who achieved various degrees of enlightenment have left descriptions of their methods and experiences. Few appear to have reached higher levels of awareness without undergoing the severest trials.

Yet it is precisely at this point that we encounter one of Maharishi's profoundest insights. This concerns the nature of desire. For almost all religious teachers, Eastern and Western, the abandonment of desire has been the means to union. Maharishi questions the assumption upon which this precept is based: the incompatibility of Absolute and relative. They are, he holds, not incompatible but complementary.

The idea that they are incompatible stems from too much insistence on one aspect of the Absolute-relative paradox (see Chapter VII): the *separateness* of God and the world. To redress the balance we must look to the other apect: the *identity* of God and the world. All this *is* That. Hence desire for anything at all is, at its deepest ('subtlest') level a desire for the Absolute.

The clarity with which this truth is perceived, and hence the nature of desire, depends on the level of consciousness of the desirer. (As usual, it is the level of consciousness which determines the outward manifestation; never the other way round.)

Stated thus baldly, the idea may sound paradoxical. But if we look at it in the proper context it will, I think, come to seem not merely reasonable but almost self-evident. To show this I must first summarize the consequences which follow from the conventional understanding.

This understanding has given rise to two not entirely distinct errors: in relation to meditation, and in relation to everyday living. As regards meditation, it is generally agreed that the highest form consists in reaching a state where all thought and feeling have been abandoned. It therefore seems that the right way to meditate is to try, in one way or another, to 'empty the mind'. I have already discussed this misconception in Chapter III, and shall not return to it here, except to reiterate that the basic mistake is to confuse the outcome of successful meditation with the means of achieving this outcome.

On the level of behaviour the same error is repeated. The enlightened man—the man in cosmic consciousness—experiences the Self as separate from activity; as a result he is equable in joy or sorrow, and he is not constantly tormented by unfulfilled desires. Unenlightened people therefore strive to think, talk, and act like the enlightened, in the belief that this will raise them to the same level of awareness. Once again the end is taken for the means.

In the past the attempt to produce enlightenment by modifying behaviour has taken various forms. Common to all, however, was the aim of 'mortification'. 'The spirit is willing, but the flesh is weak.' To strengthen the flesh the would-be contemplative embarked on a course of systematic training in spiritual athleticism. At its grossest level (I am using the words 'gross' and 'subtle' in the sense defined in Chapter III) this consisted in the adoption of physical austerities such as self-flagellation and the wearing of louse-ridden hairshirts. At certain periods, such as the Middle Ages, practices of this kind were taken as almost automatic guarantees of sanctity. Nevertheless, many authorities, including the Buddha, condemned them as ineffective and undesirable, and instead enjoined psychological mortification. As Aldous Huxley put it: 'Mortification or deliberate dying to self is inculcated with an uncompromising firmness in the canonical writings of Christianity, Hinduism, Buddhism and most of the other major and minor religions of the world, and by every theocentric saint and spiritual reformer who has ever lived out and expounded the principle of the Perennial Philosophy.' (*The Perennial Philosophy*, Chatto, 1946, pp. 106–7.) This seems clear enough. And at times the doctrine looks heartless. Even love of family must, it appears, be abandoned. (See *The Perennial Philosophy*, p. 115.) Hence the trend towards monasticism: it seemed logical that the way of the recluse should be the ideal to be aimed at by anyone seeking spiritual growth.

It is perhaps true to say that the West, with its Christian doctrine of the redemptive value of suffering, has laid more emphasis on the importance of cheerfully accepting the crosses of everyday life, whereas the East has paid more attention to cultivating detachment. This is of course a generalization, and many exceptions, in both cases, can be found. However, the profound influence of the Upanishads undoubtedly led Indians to greater extremes of detachment than were commonly found in the West—where, after all, the Quietists were declared heretical. In India attempts were made to attack the cycle of impression, recognition-desire, and action at various points, in the belief that once it was broken enlightenment would follow. Sometimes action was singled out, though clearly an even partial abstention from activity is possible only for the recluse. This is stressed in the Bhagavad Gita: 'No one, indeed, can exist even for an instant without performing action; for everyone is helplessly driven to activity by the gunas born of nature. He who sits, restraining the organs of action, and dwelling in his mind on the objects of sense, self-deluded, he is said to be a hypocrite.' (*BG*, III, 5–6.) More often the villain was taken to be desire; this is a central feature of Buddhism, at least in the form in which it has come down to us. At other times an attack was made on the senses in the belief that by reducing impressions to a minimum there would be less stimulus to desire. Again, the reading of descriptions of cosmic consciousness led some people to try to maintain 'self-awareness' on the psychological level by holding the thought 'I am seeing' along with the experience of seeing.

Such practices have not been common in the West. Instead, the Christian mystics' emphasis on the personal aspect of God led them to give more importance to 'love' as a means to union. And since it is the Christian mystics who will be most familiar to Western readers, I shall devote most of my space to them.

I have already mentioned that Abbot Chapman's 'contemplative prayer' has some resemblance to transcendental meditation, in that it does not stress concentration. There is, however, a curious difference. Chapman holds that the only people who should, or indeed can, practise contemplative prayer are those who have become unable to 'meditate' (that is, to ponder imaginatively on the truths of religion, the life of Christ, and so on). In this he is closely following St John of the Cross, who gives three signs which must, he says, be present before contemplation begins. These are inability to meditate, inability to use the imagination, and (most important) the longing to be alone with the attention 'fixed lovingly' on God without the use of the intellect. (See *The Ascent of Mount Carmel*, Book III, Chapter 13.)

It is this inability to 'meditate', Chapman believes, which constitutes the 'Night of the Senses'. What happens is that beginners start by meditating (in the sense just defined) and experience emotion—at first, with difficulty, later more easily. After some time, however, 'meditation' becomes first difficult, then nauseous, and finally impossible. This is the 'Night of the Senses' and it is the signal for contemplative prayer to begin.[1]

The difference between Chapman and Maharishi is that Chapman insists that 'contemplation' can only begin *after* love is established, whereas Maharishi sees 'contemplation' (transcendental meditation) as the path *to* love. Yet I think the difference is more apparent than real. Chapman is doubtless right in saying that the 'Night of the Senses' is a necessary preliminary to the form of prayer he describes, but that is because the efficacy of this technique is limited. Transcendental meditation is so simple and yet so effective that anyone, whatever his state of development, can begin it without preparation of any kind.

Moreover, Chapman certainly realized that 'contemplation' in itself produces the very effects which are generally seen as the means of spiritual progress. Thus he writes: 'For those who are able to practise this prayer . . . interior mortification becomes as easy as it was before difficult. . . . The real value of prayer can be securely estimated by its effect on the rest of the day. It ought to produce very definite results.' Among these is 'the cessation of multiple resolutions. We used to make and remake our resolutions, never keeping them for long. Now we make only one, to do and suffer God's Will—and we keep all our old ones, or rather, they seem to keep themselves without any trouble on our part.' Also, 'there are *flashes of the infinite*—it is difficult to

[1] St John has also a 'Night of the Spirit'. This comes on after the 'Night of the Senses' is established. Its severity and duration vary from person to person, and so does the form; today, according to Chapman, it usually appears as a feeling that religion is untrue rather than, as in the older literature, a belief that God has abandoned one. In any case, whatever its form, 'the more terrible and black the darkness, the greater the purification, and the closer the union with God.' (*SL*, pp. 147–8.) There are obvious similarities between this account and clinical descriptions of depression. I suspect that this 'Night' is related to 'nadir' experiences in the same way that peak experiences and prolonged ecstatic states are related. In other words, the 'Night of the Spirit' is a prolonged and drastic personality earthquake.

find an expression for this—when for an instant a conception passes, like lightning, of reality, eternity, etc.' (*SL*, p. 291.)

Thus, for the contemplative, as for the meditator, good behaviour becomes more and more automatic. Even the seeking of God is to be seen in this light: 'anxiety to get and to keep the sense of God's Presence or tranquillity of mind is one of the chief causes of desolation.' (*SL*, p. 174.) And even more remarkably: '*Abandon*,[1] humility, charity, those are virtues; anxiety, self-dissection, wondering what God means, wanting to know whether we are making progress, these are very nearly vices.'[2] (*SL*, p. 178.)

It seems to me that in these passages Chapman is feeling after the idea of cosmic consciousness. He comes even closer to it when he says: 'The real "I" is the will which gives itself to God, (the emotions and imaginations are not *me*, they are in me, but are not under my control); feelings come and go; but my whole business is to concentrate my will on God. That is pure charity.'[3] (*SL*, pp. 175–6.)

Why does Chapman insist on this sequence of events? I think the answer is given when he says: 'The object of meditation is to arrive at loving. Of course, love does not consist in feeling. . . .' (*SL*, p. 178.) For Chapman, love is the motive power in contemplation, and without it nothing can be done. The same point is stressed over and over again by Evelyn Underhill. 'The business and method of Mysticism is Love. Here is one of the distinctive notes of true mysticism; marking it off from every other kind of transcendental theory and practice. . . .' But, she points out, 'the word Love as applied to the mystics is to be understood in its deepest, fullest sense; as the ultimate expression of the self's most vital tendencies, not as the affection or emotion often dignified by this name. Mystic love is a total dedication of the will; the deep-seated desire and tendency of the soul towards its Source.' (*Mysticism*, p. 85.)

I find this a little contradictory. On the one hand we are told that love is not an affection or emotion; on the other, the only

---

[1] Chapman is using '*abandon*' in the French sense.

[2] Compare the Bhagavad Gita: 'The all-pervading intelligence does not accept the sin or even the merit of anyone. Wisdom is veiled by ignorance. Thereby creatures are deluded.' (V, 15.)

[3] In the sense used by St Paul, of course; it has nothing to do with alms-giving.

way of bringing it into being seems to be Chapman's 'meditation'—but this appears to generate only emotion. However, since 'contemplation' will not work unless 'love' is present, it seems that the only people who can contemplate are those who are disposed to it by nature. (I think that both Chapman and Miss Underhill might well agree that this is, in fact, the case.)

Now Maharishi seems to ignore the need for 'love' as a preliminary, and for people familiar with the literature of Christian mysticism this may be puzzling and even disconcerting. Zaehner, like Evelyn Underhill, frequently refers to Ruysbroeck's condemnations of the Quietists for being content to find perfect tranquillity within themselves (that is, in transcendental consciousness). 'And therefore,' says Ruysbroeck, 'all those men are deceived whose intention it is to sink themselves into natural rest, and who do not seek God with desire nor find Him in delectable love. For the rest which they possess consists in an emptying of themselves, to which they are inclined by nature and by habit. And in this natural rest men cannot find God.' (*The Spiritual Espousals*, tr. Eric Colledge, London, pp. 166–7.)

Transcendental consciousness, Ruysbroeck seems to be saying here, is not the highest possible state. The highest experience is theistic mysticism, and to mistake transcendental consciousness for this is to debar oneself from true religious experience. 'In Christian mysticism love is all-important, and it must be so, since God himself is defined as Love.' (*MSP*, p. 172.) Similar trends towards theistic devotion, less perfectly developed, are, Zaehner says, to be found in Islam and Hinduism.

Now Maharishi is in agreement with much of this. He, too, insists that even cosmic consciousness is not the highest state; one of the purposes of the Bhagavad Gita is to prevent people from thinking that it is. For Maharishi, as for the Christian mystics, 'devotion' is the means by which one rises from cosmic consciousness to God consciousness. However—and this is most important—Maharishi emphasizes repeatedly that the 'love' of which Zaehner speaks can only have real meaning *if it arises on the basis of cosmic consciousness*. Cosmic consciousness is full and permanent Self-awareness. Until I know *myself*, all my experiences lack a foundation. To gauge the height of a mountain one must know sea level. Maharishi insists that the reason why the experiences of higher states of consciousness described in the mystical literature so often seem to be unstable, coming and going over long periods, is that they have not arisen on the basis of cosmic consciousness.

Hence, for Maharishi, love is not the way to 'contemplation'; contemplation is the way to love. 'Love', in the sense of the word used by Evelyn Underhill and Chapman, can be a reality only in cosmic consciousness.

Once cosmic consciousness has been gained, however, love does become the motive power of further development: 'The records that history has brought us of the direct communion of saints and sages with God reveal their blessed lives, but the secret of the success of such lives lay in their transcending the fields of thought, emotion, and experience. The secret of God-realization lies in transcending the thought of God. Thought that remains thought obscures God-consciousness. Emotions likewise hide the blessed bliss. The thought of God finds fulfilment in its own extinction. And emotion too has to cease in order to let the heart be full in the unbounded love of God.

'The state of consciousness that knows the glory of the great Lord of all beings is divine. It is developed through constant and regular practice of meditation and the experience of transcendental Being, which eventually brings cosmic consciousness, the state in which the heart and mind are fully matured. This full development of the capacities of heart and mind enables a man to understand and live the divine Being. The relationship that exists between the unmanifested Absolute and the manifested Being unfolds itself. The personal God comes to be experienced on the sensory level. He becomes the living Reality of daily life. Every object in creation reflects the light of God in terms of one's own Self.' (*BG*, VI, 30, Commentary.)

The implication of all this is, I would say, that Maharishi has not introduced a radically new principle; rather, he has clarified and systematized what the Christian mystics have been talking about. Whatever a man's state, he can begin the practice of transcendental meditation. This will lead him, first to subtler states of awareness, and then to the field of the transcendent. Throughout this process his capacity for 'love' is growing; and when he reaches cosmic consciousness this capacity has unfolded to its fullest extent. Now, and only now, does the 'total dedication of the will' have meaning.

Another aspect of Maharishi's teaching that often puzzles people is his attitude to desire. Far from regarding it as a barrier to spiritual progress, he thinks of it as an essential means of fulfilment. In the light of Evelyn Underhill's 'deep-seated desire and tendency of the soul towards its Source' one can, I think, see why this should be so.

According to Stace, the implication of mysticism is that *all* desire is ultimately desire for the Absolute. This, he believes, was Plato's teaching. 'Important passages in his writings suggest that the Good, the *summum bonum*, is that which "every soul possesses as the end of all her actions, dimly divining its existence, but perplexed and unable to grasp its nature." (*The Republic*.) In *The Symposium*, putting the words into the mouth of Diotima, he asks: "What is the cause, Socrates, of love and the attendant desire? See you not how all animals, birds as well as beasts, in their desire of procreation are in an agony when they take the infection of love? . . . Why should animals have these passionate feelings? [It is because] love is of the immortal . . . the mortal nature seeking as far as possible to be everlasting and immortal, and this is attained only by generation because generation always leaves behind a new existence in place of the old." The source of all appetition, whether in men or in animals, is the hunger for the Immortal, the Good, the One.' (*MP*, p. 328.)

To trace the longing for the Absolute down even into the behaviour of animals may seem fanciful, especially in a behaviouristically-minded age like ours. Yet on the assumption that everything in creation is a manifestation of the Absolute this is what we must do. I have already discussed (pp. 86–90) the idea that consciousness is a reflection of the Absolute pure awareness in the individual nervous system, and that consequently animals presumably have their own form of consciousness. Certainly this is the view of W. H. Thorpe, who says: 'While . . . we cannot give final proof of consciousness in animals, we can bring evidence to bear which is cumulatively highly impressive and does, I believe, give powerful reasons for concluding that consciousness is a widespread feature of animal life.' (*BCE*, p. 475.) And Thorpe goes on to show that there is evidence for the existence in birds and mammals of the manipulation of abstract ideas, self-awareness, aesthetic values, and even ethical values.

In the light of mystical experience, *all* love is 'a dim groping towards that disappearance of individuality in the Universal Self which is part of the essence of mysticism.' (*MP*, p. 329.) This, I think, explains the well-known tendency of the Christian (and Sufi) mystics to use the language of sexual love and marriage as a metaphor for the union of the soul with God.[1] Richard of St Victor, for example, divides union with the Absolute into four stages, which he calls betrothal, marriage, wedlock, and the fruitfulness of the soul. (See Evelyn Underhill, *Mysticism*, pp. 139–40.)

One of the most beautiful expressions of the idea that all love is ultimately love of the One is that to be found in the Brihadaranyaka Upanishad. Here we learn that 'it is not for the love of a husband that a husband is dear, but for the love of the Soul in the husband that a husband is dear.' This is repeated for wife, children, riches, religion, creatures, and finally the All. And the conclusion is: 'It is the Soul, the Spirit, the Self, that must be seen and be heard and have our thoughts and meditation. . . . When the Soul is seen and heard, is thought upon and becomes known, then all that is becomes known.'

I have already mentioned that Maharishi has sometimes been reproached by people with a conventional religious background (and even by some without) for his apparent endorsement of hedonism. I think we are now in a position to see the deeper meaning of his teaching. If, as the whole of the mystical tradition so strongly implies (and the passage from the Brihadaranyaka

---

[1] This tendency has probably encouraged medical materialists, such as Leuba, in their belief that much if not all mystical experience is essentially the result of frustrated sexual desire. This theory has been, I think, conclusively disproved by Marghanita Laski's researches. (See *Ecstasy*, pp. 145 *et seq.*) However, Miss Laski does believe that the celibacy of most Christian mystics is the reason for their frequent employment of imagery derived from sexual love. This does not seem likely to me for two reasons. First, the mystics use this imagery, not so much to describe 'ecstasy' itself (as Miss Laski implies), but to illustrate the steps that lead up to the 'unitive life'. Secondly, it is not true, as she claims, that such imagery is confined to celibate mystics; it is one of the most characteristic features of Persian mystical poetry, but celibacy has never been a feature of Sufism. (See Arberry, *Sufism*, pp. 84–5.)

Upanishad explicitly states), all desire is ultimately desire for the Absolute, what is the purpose of trying to frustrate it? Love of possession, in particular, is often adduced as an example of a desire which is quite incompatible with spiritual aspirations, and certainly there are passages in the New Testament which seem to imply this. (The Old Testament, of course, tended to look upon riches as signs of God's approbation.) If that is the real meaning of these passages—and it has been disputed—I can only say that for me, at least, the Upanishadic recognition of the love of the divine even in the love of riches represents a more profound understanding.

I do not mean to say that love of money is an endearing characteristic; quite the contrary. But I find it quite convincing to say that the way to spirituality lies, not through frustrating and repressing even this love, but through using it constructively. For this reason transcendental meditation has universal relevance; whatever a man's aims, he will achieve them more easily if he meditates.

Yet this in no way negates the spirituality of the process. For as one meditates the desires progressively 'refine' themselves; the meditator begins to recognize that it is indeed for the sake of the Soul that riches are dear. Hence to see Maharishi's teaching as 'lowering spiritual standards' to accommodate the weakness of modern unregenerate man is a total mistake. On the contrary, Maharishi's policy is to take even the basest metal that he finds to hand with the aim of transmuting it into the finest gold.

# CHAPTER XII

## *A Vision of Possibilities*

IN THIS CONCLUDING chapter I should like to try to place Maharishi's teaching in a wider context than I have done hitherto, and to show why I believe it to be of such unique importance today.

The predominant mood of our time, reflected in much of our literature, art and music, is one of despair. 'There have been ages of pessimism in the past,' wrote M. I. Finley in a recent review in *The Listener* (28th January, 1971), 'but nothing comparable, I think, in the West since the end of the Middle Ages.' The reasons are seemingly not hard to find. Many scientists— our modern prophets—are saying that the world is close to, or even has already passed, the point of no return, and that before the end of the century we are bound to succumb to a combination of war, pollution, famine, disease, and the psychological effects of overcrowding.

Their pessimism may well be justified. It may be that civilizations of the size and complexity of ours are inherently unstable and are bound to explode, rather as stars of a certain size necessarily become novas. If this is the case there is of course nothing we can do about it. And certain signs suggest that it is; I am thinking particularly of the growth of national and international anarchy, of the apparent longing among some of the young to destroy for destruction's sake. 'Those whom Zeus would ruin. . . .' But even if the existence of a collective 'death wish' be discounted, the sheer instability of our civilization seems likely to cause its downfall.

Undoubtedly there is ample cause for gloom. Yet even now the problems which face us are not insuperable, and I believe that the real cause of our pessimism is not the objective difficulties, which are probably as much symptoms as causes of our loss of nerve; the real trouble is a failure of confidence in *ourselves*. In a recent radio programme (2nd June, 1972) the Nobel prizewinner Jacques Monod, a self-confessed pessimist, laid weight on the importance of people's philosophical attitudes to the question of life's purpose. The difficulty of changing these attitudes was for him an additional source of anxiety.

The type of change Monod seeks would, one gathers from his writings (see *Chance and Necessity*, Collins, 1972) be an acceptance of a bleak and ultra-rationalist creed, and he is clearly right in thinking that it will have little popular appeal. Its cornerstone is the scientific principle of *objectivity*, which implies that to look for a purpose in existence is unjustifiable because life is ultimately the product of blind chance. The function of religions, Monod believes, has been to provide mythologies to explain the purpose behind the universe which man instinctively seeks. The message of science is that no purpose exists. The spiritual sickness of modern man comes from his willingness to profit from the material benefits science brings without accepting its ethical consequences—that the scientific principle does indeed destroy all 'mythologies', religious or philosophical, which purport to detect a plan in the universe.

For my part, I must admit to being one of those who cannot help but hold to some version, however tentative, of the view which Monod castigates. I cannot but believe that the universe forms, in some incomprehensible way, a totality of which we are part, even though all our mythologies and systems of metaphysics fail to grasp more than the tiniest fragment of the whole. And I suspect that my belief has its origins in temperament. It seems to me that people can roughly be divided into two groups as regards their attitude to this question. On the one hand there are those one might call the Aristotelians, of whom Monod would be a good example; they welcome every piece of evidence which seems to support what Koestler has called a 'reductionist' position. On the other there are the Platonists, who tend to look below the surface of life for what they are convinced must lie hidden there. Though largely a Platonist myself, I am also aware of the valuable service which the Aristotelians perform in forcing one to think clearly and to take account of *all* the facts and not merely those one happens to like. As so often in life, both groups are partly right and partly wrong. The Platonists are primarily concerned with *subjective* reality, the Aristotelians with *objective* reality. Both are valid approaches; what is needed is common ground on which they can meet.

Now I believe that transcendental meditation and its underlying philosophy offer the prospect of a reconciliation between the two groups, since they afford a means of exploring the inner world which is reliable and reproducible and also a coherent and intellectually satisfying framework to contain the discoveries of that exploration. A reconciliation between Platonists and Aristotelians was never more needed than it is today, when disillusionment with science and its fruits seems to be causing an extraordinary outburst of irrationalism that finds popular expression in such phenomena as the current revival of interest in witchcraft, astrology, numerology and similar occultisms. It is easy to adopt a supercilious attitude to these trends, but we should not deceive ourselves; they pose a real danger. Almost certainly they represent a sign of the continuing need of man for religion; but they are a perversion of the true religious instinct, and are signs of sickness rather than health. Nor should we underestimate their power; like a fungus cracking a slab of concrete by the slow relentless pressure of its growth, the anti-rationalism of our time may yet bring down science in ruin. Polanyi has warned that science as we know it may be dead in fifty years. And I do not think that anyone, even the most ardent of Platonists, should be indifferent to this. Whether we like science or not, we cannot destroy it and hope to preserve our civilization. As Merleau-Ponty is reported to have said recently, 'ou la science ou la barbarie.'

In any case, to think of science as the enemy of spirituality is a mistake. Maharishi sees life as a constant seeking for fulfilment, and the Western quest for knowledge as the prime modern instance of this. He will therefore have no truck with proposals to cut down the rate of progress in the 'relative field'. The very kernel of his teaching, after all, is that material and spiritual values of life, far from being mutually exclusive, are intimately bound up with each other.

I am sure he is right in this; but it also seems to me that we shall have to redefine our values and our concept of 'progress' if we are to survive at all. From now on, true progress will consist more and more in living in conformity with Albert Schweitzer's principle of 'reverence for life'. We shall have to recognize in what sense we are in truth a part of nature. This will mean having more wisdom and less cleverness—in a word, eliminating our fatal tendency to *hubris*.

Many young people in the West have recently been showing signs of a growing disillusion with technology, competitiveness, and the whole notion of 'progress', and have been looking, sometimes in unlikely places, for 'spiritual' satisfaction. It is easy to sneer at this idealism and to say that the young people in question would not indulge in these flights of fancy if their bellies were not filled by the technology they profess to despise. Perhaps so; but I think that their instinct is right. They are, after all, only learning by experience the truth of Christ's saying that man does not live by bread alone. Most of us are still at the stage of endless searching in the relative world for what cannot be found there—permanent happiness. If our society as a whole could discover that a reliable means of establishing inner peace existed there would be a shift in its centre of gravity towards the Absolute value of life that would permit us to make whatever adjustments on the relative plane proved to be necessary.

To say this is not to advocate a world-denying asceticism. The relative world is there to be enjoyed; but it seems to me self-evident that changes in our present way of life are coming whether we like it or not. If he is to survive at all, man will have to change and evolve. Many people have said this, of course, and many solutions have been proposed, ranging from the conventionally religious (repentance) to the pharmacological (Koestler's idea of an 'anti-aggression' drug). To assign one cause, and one cure, to our present ills may well seem an enormous over-simplification. There is a natural human tendency to seek over-facile solutions; how many would-be prophets in the past have promised the millennium if only people would heed them? Yet if, as I believe we must, we accept the validity of the mystics' claim that all of the phenomenal world stems ultimately from the Absolute, there *can* be only one solution to our difficulties: to go back to the Absolute.

This may sound excessively 'mystical'. Is it conceivable that human nature in the mass can really become any different from what it is now? I frankly do not know. Undoubtedly the practice of transcendental meditation does seem to alter people, but whether it will spread widely enough and act quickly enough is another question. However, perhaps this way of looking at the problem is too superficial. Let me explain.

I have come to believe strongly that our ordinary view of life is 'two-dimensional'. What we usually take to be the whole of life is in reality merely the outermost layer; it is like a thin film of oil floating on water. The patterns we see are produced by hidden shiftings at great depths, and our minds are moved by currents of which we know nothing.

If one looks back into history one finds from time to time widespread changes in world outlook that seem hard to account for. I am thinking particularly of the quite astonishing outflow of creativity in the late sixth century BC that gave us, within a relatively short space of time, the Upanishads, Buddhism, and the philosophy of Plato. Where do such changes originate? Historians will doubtless produce answers, and I do not wish to dispute any of the explanations which they may advance; but I am tempted to suspect that there may be more to it than is thought of in our philosophy. Broad has pointed out (*Lectures on Psychical Research*, Routledge, 1962, pp. 219–20) that telepathy, if it occurs at all, probably operates much more widely and continuously than can be proved to be the case. My state of consciousness may be modified by that of other people who are unknown to me, or my behaviour may be influenced without any introspectable change in my state of consciousness—a sort of telepathic subliminal advertising.

Perhaps such an idea seems utterly fantastic. However, the concept of 'psychic contagion', as it has been called, would help to explain otherwise puzzling phenomena such as the 'miracle' of Fatima, in which many (but not all) of the members of a crowd of thousands 'saw' the sun perform fantastic gyrations and finally come hurtling down upon them. On a less dramatic but ultimately more important level it would help to account for the almost simultaneous emergence of new ideas in different parts of the world which I have mentioned. And it would suggest a conception of our individual minds as islands, apparently separate but in reality joined together beneath the sea, that is in line with the view of the Self which I have been putting forward in this book.

If such a view of man be accepted, it becomes possible to believe that, as Maharishi claims, the spread of transcendental meditation will have wide and profound effects on the world's mental climate. The quality of thought of meditators, being 'subtler' than usual, would have more effect telepathically than the ordinary 'gross' thought; and since such subtle thought is, by definition, more blissful, more imbued with the peace of the Absolute, it would have the effect of calming the bellicosity and tensions of the world at large. William James would, I think, have had no difficulty in accepting this notion.

'The further limits of our being plunge us, it seems to me, into an altogether other dimension of existence from the sensible and merely "understandable" world. . . . So far as our ideal impulses originate in this region (and most of them do originate in it, for we find them possessing us in a way for which we cannot articulately account), we belong to it in a more intimate sense than that in which we belong to the visible world, for we belong in the most intimate sense wherever our ideals belong. Yet the unseen region in question is not merely ideal, for it produces effects in this world. When we commune with it, work is actually done upon our finite personality, for we are turned into new men, and consequences in the way of conduct follow in the natural world upon our regenerative change. But that which produces effects within another reality must be termed a reality itself, so I feel as if we had no philosophical excuse for calling the unseen or mystical world unreal.' (*VRE*, pp. 490–1.)

This remarkable passage comes from the Conclusion to James' great study, and it is a measure of James' stature that he was prepared to state his position so uncompromisingly. Yet there is, as he acknowledges in a postscript, a certain difficulty outstanding. What *precise* difference does the unseen mystical world make to our everyday one? How does its influence make itself felt? Here the best that James can offer is the notion that God produces his effects in our world by 'incursions from the subconscious region'.

So far as it goes, I am sure that this is true. But these invasions are sporadic and uncontrollable; we cannot make full use of them. We are like primitive man before he mastered the art of making fire; it cannot have been very satisfactory to have to wait for the forest to be ignited by lightning before you could warm yourself or cook a meal. Hitherto we have had to wait for the spontaneous incursions which we call conversion, or mystical experience, or ecstasy; they were totally unpredictable. Now, however, it seems that we have in transcendental meditation the possibility of a controlled, continuous release of 'spiritual' energy.

And yet, what does all this mean in practice? I am sometimes asked what I have 'got out of' practising transcendental meditation; it is a fair question, yet it is surprisingly difficult to answer. Everyone naturally starts meditating at a different stage of development, and many people could undoubtedly speak with far greater insight and authority about meditation's benefits. Furthermore, in talking about the effects of meditation, again and again one comes up against their apparent ordinariness. I have mentioned this before, but it is worth stressing once again. Meditation produces a *natural* growth of the personality, and so as the various 'higher' states of consciousness develop they are *not* typically experienced as strange or surprising; more often they are felt to be the *normal* state of awareness—which, of course, they are. Hence to expect accounts of bizarre experiences from meditators would be a mistake; such experiences are not the rule, and in any case are not essential to progress. Indeed, it appears that the longer one meditates the smaller becomes the contrast between one's 'ordinary' state and the 'higher' states.

For my part, I would say that the greatest gain I have had from meditation is something which is remarkably hard to put into words. Perhaps I can best illustrate it by a practical example. Before I meditated I used to be appalled by the thought of death. Now, so far as I can discover by introspection, this is no longer so. As far as I can tell I am curious about death but not afraid of it except in so far as it may entail suffering. Yet this loss of the fear of death is not, I think, related to any new-found certainty about survival;[1] rather, it is part of a general increase in what

[1] Although Maharishi accepts the usual Indian idea of reincarnation (which, of course, is easily fitted into the tripartite scheme of personality), he seldom talks about it. Like the Buddha, who apparently held that speculation on such matters was not conducive to enlightenment, he prefers to concentrate on the here and now; to be born as a human being is, he says, an extraordinarily valuable opportunity that must not be lost. It seems as if the evolution of the personality can only be achieved by acting on its grossest manifestation, the physical body.

perhaps can best be described as a sense of inner security and stability. This is not to say that the vicissitudes of life no longer affect me; far from it. Paradoxically, there seems to be an increase in sensitivity but a decrease in the liability to be thrown off balance by sudden changes in fortune, good or bad. On the intellectual level many questions remain; but increasingly I come to see that the way to resolve them is not by reading or discussion but rather by deepening one's awareness through meditation. 'Knowing this, let the lover of Brahman follow wisdom. Let him not ponder on many words, for many words are weariness.'

The increase in a sense of security is what Maharishi speaks of as the growth of Being within the Self, and it seems to be the regular experience of meditators. It is this which is the real justification of meditation.

At bottom our problem in life, it seems to me, is always the same: fear. Fear of death, fear of illness, fear of old age, fear of pain, fear of war—the list is endless. What is the source of fear? The Upanishads say: 'Fear comes from a second.' Here, surely, is the key to the abolition of fear.

The man who has achieved full enlightenment has come to see that his Self is present in everything. In this state of awareness there can be no 'second' and hence no fear. The Spirit, the Upanishads declare, is beyond suffering and fear:

'Who knows this and has found peace, he is the Lord of himself, his is a calm endurance, and calm concentration. In himself he sees the Spirit, and he sees the Spirit as all. . . .

'. . . This is the Spirit of the universe, a refuge from all fear.'

# APPENDIX

# Appendix

IN THE LAST few years a number of physiological studies of transcendental meditation have been carried out, and as a result it can be said that the meditation produces a physiological state which is clearly distinguishable from the waking, dreaming, and dreamless sleep states[1] as well as from abnormal states such as hypnotic trance.

The most extensive studies so far undertaken have been those reported by Wallace, Benson, and Wilson[2] at Thorndyke Memorial Laboratory, Harvard Medical School.

The principal results were as follows:

1. Oxygen consumption fell by about 17% almost as soon as meditation began; this fall is as large as that which occurs after several hours' sleep.
2. The carbon dioxide and oxygen partial pressures in arterial blood did not change significantly, so the fall in oxygen consumption was not associated with either carbon dioxide retention or anoxia to any significant extent.
3. Blood lactate levels fell significantly during meditation and remained low for the short period of observation after meditation; hence anaerobic processes were apparently not involved. This finding is also of interest in another way: some recent studies have suggested that intravenous infusion of lactate can cause anxiety attacks in susceptible individuals and even in some normal people. It therefore seems possible that the ability of transcendental meditation to relieve anxiety subjectively can be related to an objective biochemical change.
4. Cardiac output fell during meditation by an average of about 25%.
5. Galvanic skin resistance rose markedly during meditation— by as much as 500% in some cases.

[1] Kleitman, N., *Sleep and Wakefulness*, Chicago, 1963.
[2] Wallace, R. K.; Benson, H.; Wilson, A. F., *American Journal of Physiology*, 1971, vol. 221, p. 795.

6. The electro-encephalogram showed interesting features. Alpha rhythm, present in all subjects at rest, increased during meditation in both regularity and amplitude. In some subjects the alpha activity occasionally stopped for two to five minutes and was replaced by low-voltage theta waves. Alpha blocking caused by repeated sound or light stimuli showed no habituation. I have already pointed out (p. 60) the ways in which these findings resemble, and differ from, the findings in Zen meditation.

It is important to understand that these results cannot reasonably be attributed to suggestion; oxygen consumption does not fall consistently during hypnosis and falls of the magnitude recorded during transcendental meditation cannot be explained in this way. Reviewing the findings of Wallace and his associates, the *Lancet* commented: 'An immediate reduction in oxygen consumption consistently related to a mental process is remarkable, and the mechanism is entirely obscure.' (Editorial, 1972, 1, p. 1058.)

As the *Lancet* also points out, the true reduction in oxygen consumption was almost certainly greater than that recorded in these experiments, since the apparatus used to measure it inevitably interfered with the subjects' meditation. This difficulty was partially overcome by J. Allison, who in an earlier study was able to record very shallow respirations at rates down to four per minute. (*Lancet*, 1970, 1, p. 833.) Even in these experiments, however, the apparatus was sufficiently obtrusive to act as a distraction, and indeed the mere awareness that breathing was being measured was enough to upset meditation; thus the true fall in breathing volume and rate (and hence in oxygen consumption) was probably greater still.

*The psychological effects of transcendental meditation*
To obtain objective evidence that the meditation produces psychological benefits is clearly much harder than to demonstrate its physiological effects, since the influence of suggestion is hard to rule out. However, work on these lines is already under way at several centres, mainly in the USA. Dr Benson

gave retrospective questionnaires to 1,800 people taking part in residential courses to train as teachers of the meditation; 80% admitted to having used hashish previously, whereas after meditating for some months the great majority had ceased to take the drug. Similar results were found for other drugs, including narcotics. As Benson points out, this study has little validity, being retrospective; however, a large-scale prospective study is now under way and its results will be most interesting.

A number of other studies of a preliminary nature have been carried out. D. W. Orme-Johnson, of the University of Texas at El Paso, has produced evidence that meditation stabilizes autonomic function. He used habituation of the galvanic skin response to a loud sound as a measure of stability, and found significant differences between meditators and controls as regards rate of habituation. In one typical experiment, the skin response of the meditators had fallen to zero by about fifteen minutes, whereas the non-meditators had a much slower fall and were still showing some response at forty minutes. At the University of Cincinnati Shostram's Personal Orientation Inventory was given to fifteen people two days before they learned to meditate. Two months later the tests were repeated; twenty non-meditators acted as controls on each occasion. For six of the twelve variables measured, the meditating group showed significant gains in 'self-actualization'. (Information on both studies by personal communication.)

## Medical Applications

Transcendental meditation is not primarily a therapy; it is meant to make 'normal' people more normal! However, the physiological characteristics of the meditative state have suggested to a number of workers that it might be useful in the prevention or treatment of various diseases. So far little has been published on this, although the studies by Wallace *et al.* showed that significant reductions in arterial blood pressure occurred during and for some time after periods of meditation. Benson is currently investigating the possibility of using transcendental meditation therapeutically in essential hypertension. (Information by personal communication.)

In a recent paper entitled *Mystical States of Consciousness:*

*Neurophysiological and Clinical Aspects* (Journal of Nervous and Mental Disease, 1972, vol. 154, p. 399), E. Gellhorn and W. F. Kiely wrote:

'There is reason to believe that transcendental meditation, an easily learned technique in contrast to the rigorous training involved in Zen and Yoga exercises, may be useful clinically in the treatment of psychosomatic tension states, anxiety, and phobic reactions. Its application in the therapy of disorders such as essential hypertension, bronchial asthma, "brittle" juvenile diabetes mellitus, and a number of other psychosomatic disorders would likewise suggest itself.'

# Postscript

TRANSCENDENTAL meditation is taught throughout the world by teachers all of whom have been personally trained by Maharishi. It is always taught individually. The usual sequence of events is as follows. People are invited to an introductory talk, at which the principles of the meditation are explained and there is an opportunity to ask questions. Those interested are invited to attend a further talk, at which the practical details of learning to meditate are gone into. The next step is a personal interview with the teacher; this gives the would-be meditator a chance to ask any questions that he felt disinclined to bring out in public. At the interview an appointment is made for actually learning to meditate.

The teaching itself occupies about an hour. On the following three days the new meditator returns to his teacher—for about an hour on each occasion—for further instruction and to make sure that he has grasped the principle of meditation fully. At the end of this four-day period the teacher has imparted all the basic knowledge needed for successful practice of the technique. But of course trained teachers are always available to give further help, and it is a good idea to keep in touch with one of these from time to time.

Talks and discussions about the underlying philosophy of the meditation are held regularly, but these are in no sense compulsory. To meditate one does not have to be organized.

One important point to notice: teachers of transcendental meditation are concerned with the meditation *alone*. It is no part of their task to enquire into a person's private life or to give personal advice. A meditator's private life remains private throughout.

Practitioners of transcendental meditation are now to be found in almost every part of the world; there are teachers in the following countries, and the list is growing constantly: Argentina, Australia, Austria, Brazil, Denmark, France, West Germany, Greece, Holland, Israel, Italy, Japan, Malaysia,

New Zealand, South Africa, Sweden, Switzerland, Trinidad, Turkey, Uruguay.

The largest national centres, which can provide further information, are as follows.

*Great Britain*
The Spiritual Regeneration Movement Foundation of Great Britain,
32 Cranbourn Street,
London, W.C.2 H 7EY

*USA*
Students' International Meditation Society,
1015 Gayley Avenue,
Los Angeles,
California 90024.

*Canada*
Students' International Meditation Society,
Office 2,
840 Fort Street,
Victoria BC.

*Australia*
Transcendental Meditation Centre,
29 Drummond Street,
Carlton,
Melbourne,
Victoria 3053.

*New Zealand*
The Spiritual Regeneration Movement Foundation of New Zealand,
17 Horoeka Avenue,
Mount Eden,
Auckland 3.

*South Africa*
Spiritual Regeneration Centre,
Rossiter Street,
Tamboers Kloof,
Cape Town.


*India*
The Spiritual Regeneration Movement Foundation of India,
The Academy of Meditation,
Shankaracharya Nagar,
Rishikesh UP.

# Bibliography

The books I have referred to most frequently, and the abbreviations which I have used in doing so, are as follows:

*BCE*:   *Brain and Conscious Experience*, edited by J. C. Eccles (Berlin and New York, Springer-Verlag, 1966).

*BG*:   Maharishi Mahesh Yogi, *Bhagavad Gita, A New Translation and Commentary, Chapters 1–6* (International SRM Publications, 1967).

*Ecstasy*:   Marghanita Laski, *Ecstasy: A Study of Some Secular and Religious Experiences* (London, Cresset, 1961).

*MM*:   Erwin Schrödinger, *What is Life? Mind and Matter* (Cambridge University Press, in one volume, 1967).

*MP*:   W. T. Stace, *Mysticism and Philosophy* (London, Macmillan, 1961).

*MSP*:   R. C. Zaehner, *Mysticism Sacred and Profane* (Oxford University Press, 1957).

*SBAL*:   Maharishi Mahesh Yogi, *The Science of Being and Art of Living* (International SRM Publications, 1966).

*SL*:   *The Spiritual Letters of Dom John Chapman*, edited by Dom Roger Hudleston (London, Sheed & Ward, second edition (enlarged), 1935).

*VRE*:   William James, *The Varieties of Religious Experience* (London, Collins, 1960).

Almost any chronic illness
will kill you in the end —
if you can live that
long.